Faces, Forms, Films

Faces, Forms, Films

The Artistry of Lon Chaney

Robert G. Anderson

South Brunswick and New York: A. S. Barnes and Company
London: Thomas Yoseloff Ltd

A. S. Barnes and Co., Inc.
Cranbury, New Jersey 08512

Thomas Yoseloff Ltd
108 New Bond Street
London W1Y OQX, England

ISBN 0-498-07726-8
Printed in the United States of America

Contents

Introduction

When Lon Chaney died motion pictures lost a unique star. He was one of the most popular stars of the screen, and yet one of the least known. He hid his face with various kinds of make-up, rarely showing his true self on the screen and then only to confound those critics who claimed he was not an actor but some kind of freak or contortionist. He hid his off-screen life from the public, partly from his great desire for privacy, partly from his intense interest in his work, and partly because the publicity of being a mystery man further enhanced his screen image.

He was as unlike the popular notion of a star as he was unlike the characters he portrayed. There was, however, an essential part of himself he brought to his roles that was not entirely due to his skill as an actor. He was able to project the humanity of each character, so that whether his deformity was man-made or nature-made, he was believable to the audiences and therefore was real and evoked sympathy.

The audiences of the motion picture were composed of many different elements: the critics, the seekers of art, but mainly those who wanted to be entertained and to escape the world in which they lived. They rarely wanted realism because it was too much like the world in which they lived. For a few hours they wanted to experience a reality of the imagination, a world they could easily believe existed. So they could experience the life shown on the screen without having to participate.

7

Lon Chaney, 1883–1930.

The movies were an expression of the times: sometimes reflecting society as it was and sometimes suggesting what it should be. The country went through great changes during the period of the silent pictures. There had been a war, crime and violence stemming partly from an unpopular law, labor unrest, economic crises, scientific breakthroughs including the conquest of the air, and a relaxing of moral standards. The movies showed it all, but with an eye toward the better world of the future. Along with the realism were the escape pictures: love stories, historical romance, and high adventure. There was something for everyone.

During this period, there were many changes in the motion picture industry. It became big business, exerting great force in the economics of the country. Independent producing companies merged to become the giant studios and the products became more technically perfect. With the development of new film, cameras, lights, and with the emergence of great directors, writers, cameramen, and astute producers, motion pictures reached great heights.

At first movies were a novelty and relatively inexpensive entertainment, easily understood by the great many people to whom the language barrier denied other forms of art. Comedy and slapstick were easy to understand and the Westerns provided plenty of action. If the plots and characterization were unsubtle or nonexistent, it mattered little. As the movies became more firmly established as both industry and entertainment and attracted more sophisticated audiences, there was a demand for bigger and better pictures. So the studios began making longer movies. The sets were more elaborate, the casts were larger and had more stars, and the stories were adapted from plays and novels or written by popular authors expressly for the movies. The movie houses grew in order to accommodate the new type of picture they showed.

And then there were the stars, those personalities whose comings and goings set the emotions of their fans quivering. They were the people who brought the dollars into the box-office and whose popularity obscured the contributions of the many behind-the-scenes technicians whose constant attention to details made it possible to put a motion picture together.

Lon Chaney was one of the stars. His film career began in 1912 or 1913, in Hollywood, a few years after picture-making moved westward. In a period of eighteen years he rose from bit player to star. His career can best be divided into three parts: the beginnings—playing in slapstick comedy, Westerns, and in gangster pictures as heavies, with an occasional turn at writing and directing; the middle period—searching for an identity; and the star period.

When he entered pictures he had over twelve years of stage experience behind him, being everything from prop boy, stage hand and manager to comic and eccentric dancer. He worked during the time of the traveling stock companies whose activities centered in the West and Midwest, with Chicago as the focal point for bookings. He had never been a headliner nor hit the big time. He went into pictures primarily because he had a son to raise and was tired of traveling.

It is difficult to know how much of a man's life is the result of his own efforts and how much is attributable to the inexorable workings of fate. In this case fate was largely responsible for his being in the right place at the right time. He wasn't any kind of success and didn't have a goal except to work and keep busy. There was nothing extraordinary about him at all. He was just average: thirty years old, five feet ten inches tall, one hundred sixty pounds, dark hair and brown eyes, and full of nervous energy. There was no evidence of his latent talent or potentialities except his willingness to work. He wrote and directed some of his early films, was interested in camera work both professionally and for his own enjoyment, was intrigued with the production aspects of filming, and was especially attracted to the possibilities of make-up and characterization.

Lon Chaney was a technician, an entertainer, an actor, an artist, and a star. From backstage he moved onstage, doing comedy and song-and-dance; then from movie bits to writing and directing; and then to acting, all the while concentrating on and developing his talent for make-up and character study. His audiences grew to be frightened, shocked, awed; to sympathize with and to cheer him; to make him a star.

It is fairest to study a man and his work within the context of his own time. We look at the past with the eyes of the present and sometimes do not see reality. We look with an overcritical eye and with an emotional nostalgia, seeking on the one hand something that didn't exist and on the other something we wish did exist. The achievements of the man and the actor are difficult to assess, for there is a temptation to extend the one into the other, denying the one at the expense of the other. We can never be quite sure where the man leaves off and the actor begins.

It is not the purpose of this book to present a definitive biography, examining minutely each event or circumstance in the man's life in order to explain or interpret his actions or motivations, as interesting and dramatic as that could be. We are primarily interested in presenting the creative actor, who, through skill and craftsmanship, brought to the screen such memorable portraits. We can only look superficially at the known facts and to attempt to relate them to the aspects of his career which we examine. It is necessary to keep following the thread and not become lost in the labyrinth of the arts and sciences of the motion picture, the business of the industry, or in its social and esthetic aspects. Regrettably only a few of the many men and women who contributed to raising the movies to an art form can be mentioned in order for us to follow that thread.

Faces, Forms, Films

The Early Years

In Greek mythology the three goddesses determining the course of human life are Clotho, who spins the thread of life; Lachesis, who determines its length; and Atropos, who cuts it off; The Fates, as they are called, dealt with Alonzo Chaney much as they would the hero of a Greek tragedy. The length of the thread when cut was far too short, but it was a golden thread, bright with accomplishment and success, twisted with heartache and hardship, and interwoven with irony. No dramatist could have created a more extraordinary story: that of a man born on April Fool's Day of deaf mute parents, who learned to communicate with his hands and body, and died of throat cancer on the threshold of a new career in which he would have been able to use his expressive voice.

Lon Chaney was born April 1, 1883, at Colorado Springs, Colorado, and died August 26, 1930, in a Los Angeles, California, hospital. The second of four children, none of whom was deaf or mute; but their maternal grandmother had four children who were. Chaney's mother staged entertainments for an institution in which a three-year-old Lon appeared in charades and pantomime sketches. When he was about nine he was taken out of the fourth grade to care for his younger brother and sister and for his mother who had been stricken with inflammatory rheumatism. In order to communicate with her and relate the day's experiences he used his hands, face, and body. Thus he began to use his body much as a dancer would, to create not only situation but also mood.

In spite of this background, Chaney maintained that his childhood had not been an unhappy one and that he had indulged in his fair share of childhood games and adventures. He must have realized very early that life for him was not going to be easy and there would be hard work ahead.

His family was of very modest means; his father was a barber. Chaney once commented that this had been an unbeatable combination as his father couldn't talk to his customers and they couldn't talk back to him. His brother John worked in one of the small local theatres, and when Lon was twelve years old he worked there as a prop boy for twenty-five cents a night. During the summer months he worked as a Pike's Peak guide. His father didn't think the theatre held great promise for a future. It might be all right for one son, but he sent Lon to Denver to learn a useful trade, carpet-laying and paper-hanging. Lon was proud of this achievement, saying later that if anything happened to his acting career he could always go back to that. He was always proud of his union cards and carried his membership card in the stage hands' union until his death. Throughout his whole life he respected craftsmanship and the sense of perfection it instilled in him drove him to extend himself beyond mere necessity in order to achieve an effect that satisfied him.

But he was drawn to the theatre. He had seen the great and near great actors from backstage when they played their one and two night stands on their way across country. He was fascinated that grease paint, gesture, voice change, and carriage could transform them from one character into another. Around the turn of the century, the theatre was considered one of the prime sources of contact with the world away from home. Most cities, whether large or small, had theatres, some with their own stock companies, but most visited by traveling companies. It was in such a theatre that Lon worked backstage, mostly as a stagehand, with an occasional appearance onstage as a super. Such an atmosphere sharpened his sense of observation of people. By noting the styles of acting and characterization he was able to formulate ideas, which he later drew on in his own acting career. This restless, lithe, and energetic young man, who had learned, through necessity, to communicate by pantomime, now learned his trade well, accepting its responsibility and rigid discipline.

In 1901, John, then twenty-three, formed his own stock company and asked the eighteen-year-old Lon to join him. They wrote their

own play, *The Little Tycoon,* and produced Gilbert and Sullivan operas at the Grand Opera House. Lon played comedy roles and arranged dancing acts in addition to being an all-around stagehand. The company toured Colorado but had financial difficulties. When the tenor of the troup, Charles Holmes, offered to buy the company, John sold out, but Lon stayed on, not only taking care of transportation and wardrobe but serving as a comedian. He knew no music and couldn't sing, but comedians didn't have to have a singing voice, they just talked their songs. The only dramatic part he played was Gaspard in *The Chimes of Normandy*.

The company of twenty-three toured throughout the Midwest and South, sometimes traveling in the caboose on freight trains. It was a real luxury when they hit a town that had a theatre with dressing rooms, or that had a theatre at all. Sometimes performances were given in halls or stores. On some stages the footlights were coal-oil lamps that had a habit of going out at the most inopportune times. During the performance of one of their first plays, *Said Pasha*, the lights went out while the hero held the heroine in his arms, forcing the players to speak their lines in darkness while maneuvering toward the footlights to relight them. The troupe had its ups and downs, mostly downs. On Christmas Eve in 1903 they arrived in a small Florida town. They had no money. They made a tree and decorated it with bits and pieces from the wardrobe trunk, and Lon made caricature sketches as gifts for each member.

When the Columbia Musical Comedy Repertory Company was in Oklahoma City, a fifteen-year-old, stage-struck girl applied for a job with them. She was a lovely choir singer with a sweet voice, and Lon fell in love with her. She was overwhelmed by this confident young man who insisted he could teach her to dance, but actually never could. Three days later, after getting her mother's approval, Lon and Cleva Creighton were married. The next year, their son, Creighton, was born.

Now began a difficult period. The responsibilities of maintaining a family unit, the uncertainties of bookings, and the constant moving were a strain on the young people. Their only homes were hotel rooms in which they did their washing and cooking, while still devoting the major portion of their time to work. Nothing was permanent. When a show folded, as was often the case with small traveling troupes, they would head for Chicago, which was the booking headquarters.

Lon got a job as second comedian in *The Cowpuncher* at fourteen dollars a week. The next year he was stranded while playing in *The Beggar Prince* with a troupe in Columbus, South Carolina. William Cranston, a Canadian manager, sent them fare to Halifax, from which they were routed westward through the mining camps and on to Vancouver. The Canadian audiences had seen no plays for months and flocked to see *The Beggar Prince*. On the following tour eastward the audiences stayed away even though the company had added two new shows to the bill, *The Royal Chef* and *A Knight for a Day*. The company was again stranded but got a three-day engagement in one town, which gave them fare to head back to Chicago. They had to face the same cheap hotel rooms again. Sometimes Lon would go to the saloons, which then served free lunch with the beer, eat one sandwich and smuggle another back to the hotel for his wife.

Finally he got a job as stage manager for *The Girl in the Kimono*, in which Lee Moran was second comedian. After the show closed, Lon managed, with some help from his family, to take his wife and son to Los Angeles, where his brother was stage manager for a theatre. Going to work for a tabloid musical stock company at the Olympic theatre, he played seven shows a day, seven days a week, for $35. (Tabloids were an abbreviated version of musical comedy shows not far removed from vaudeville.) His versatility and energy gave him plenty of experience but not much money. He stayed with the company about six months and then joined the Grand Opera House Company, working with Roscoe Arbuckle, who was later to become a famous film comedian, and Robert Z. Leonard, the star baritone of the company, who went on to become a leading man in the movies and then a well-known director.

Chaney's work attracted the attention of Kolb and Dill, popular comedians of the day whose routines were similar to those of the great Joe Weber and Lew Fields. They were readying *The Rich Mr. Higgenheimer* for presentation at the Savoy theatre in San Francisco and offered Chaney the job of stage manager. He next joined Ferris Hartman's Comic Opera Company, which toured up and down the coast, appearing in *Rose of Algeria* and *Lonesome Town*. One of the members of the chorus was Hazel Bennett Hastings.

After this tour he returned to Los Angeles and sporadic employment doing comedy routines. But his wife was working steadily as a singer, and as her popularity grew and Cleva became a favorite of the cabaret set, their domestic differences started to appear. She was enjoying success, but her career was causing personal and professional jealousies. Young and pretty, and relatively inexperienced, she had found recognition easily while Lon's years of pursuing the footlights had not brought him any closer.

He insisted that she spend more time taking care of their son and her household, and this conflict resulted in Cleva's overly dramatic attempt at suicide while in the wings of a theatre during one of his performances. She was rushed to a hospital, and although Chaney stayed by her side through this crisis, after recovery was assured he left, and never went back to her.

Creighton was now his sole responsibility, and it did not solve any problems to find his present company booking a tour through the Orient. He decided it was necessary to settle down and maintain a steady income and atmosphere to raise his son properly. The movies looked as if they could meet these requirements.

The Movies—Apprenticeship

In the early days motion pictures were made mostly in the East. When a group of producers formed a combine to force the exhibitors to show only their pictures, some of the independent exhibitors rebelled at the exorbitant charges. Some film makers moved to the West Coast to escape the combine and make pictures for their own theatres. By 1912 most of the studios were located in Hollywood and the combine was all but broken. By this time, too, movies had become the accepted entertainment, replacing the traveling stock companies, which, in turn, simply moved into the new medium. The movies even lured actors and actresses from the legitimate stage as public demand forced studios to make longer four- and five-reel features rather than the one- and two-reelers, which were cheaper to make.

The exact details of how Chaney entered the movie scene are somewhat obscure, for Chaney's accounts are at variance with those of other witnesses. For instance, Al Christie, the great comedy maker, once said he first saw Lon doing a comedy routine in a burlesque house and because the show was closing gave Lon a job. His first part was that of a comic drunk who had lost his clothes and had to go home in a barrel. He said Lon stayed with him for only a year and then went to Universal. In an article Chaney wrote for *Theatre Magazine,* he stated he was stranded in Santa Ana when he heard that in Hollywood the movie studios hired men for

five dollars a day to ride horses. It seemed a great deal of pay, although he wasn't sure he could ride, but he went, and stayed, not
only on the horse, but in the movies. At any rate his early film work
at Universal was in slapstick comedy. His pay was five dollars a

day, and he worked steadily. The studio turned out countless one- and two-reelers that were made in a few days, so there was always a week's work and a paycheck. For the time being that was all that was necessary. The ambitions and direction were yet to come.

The making of these short films went at a hectic and hazardous pace. One of the production units at Universal, Gold Seal, went on location at Mt. Lowe, high above Pasadena, to shoot two two-reelers, *Bloodhounds of the North* and *The Honor of the Mounted*, both stories of the Northwest Mounted Police. Note the economy here: same costumes, same setting, same cast. They were to be there for seven days but unfortunately were caught in a heavy rainstorm and were stranded at Ye Alpine Tavern. Chaney and another cast member, Arthur Rosson, got lost in a deep canyon. Hunting parties went out but they could not locate the two men until late that night. The rain continued for five days, and when finally the weather cleared the pictures were shot in two days.

Chaney always worked hard, calling upon his past experience and knowledge of stage make-up to add a new dimension to his roles. He was listed as a lead on the roster of the production unit but rarely played a leading man. Usually he was cast as the secondary lead, or the heavy. The greatness of his talent was not yet recognized, but he was becoming known for injecting a quality into his roles that set them apart. *The Universal Weekly* of April 25, 1914, praised his portrayal in *The Tragedy of Whispering Creek*:

Mr. Chaney has used his own ideas in working out the character, a pervert, in this play, and what he has given us is startling to an unusual degree. True, he paints a horrible picture for us—one that is apt to cause a feeling of revulsion. But that is as it should be. In fact Mr. Chaney has created a NEW character—one that will live long—that will be copied as a newer standard by others.

In April of 1914 Chaney divorced Cleva and retained custody of their son. Cleva did not try to resume her singing career, her voice having been damaged by her suicide attempt. She said she never bore resentment toward Chaney, feeling perhaps much of her trouble was her own making. Chaney remarried in 1915. He had become reacquainted with Hazel Hastings, herself divorced from her crippled husband, and the two began a marriage that was to bring success and happiness to them both. Hazel devoted herself to her husband, his career, and to his son whom she brought up as her own. Young

Creighton had been led to believe that Cleva was dead, and there was a period of estrangement between Lon and his son, when Creighton later discovered that his mother was still alive.

Chaney was making about forty-five dollars a week, and besides

This scene from an early Universal film shows Chaney with false beard and moustache. Great care had to be taken not only in the application but in the selection of the proper shade of crepe hair to produce a realistic effect.

acting, directed and wrote scenarios for some one- and two-reelers. But he felt he could do his best work in front of the cameras. The studios were making longer features now that allowed for bigger roles. From 1916 to 1918 most of the films he was in were directed by Joseph DeGrasse or his wife, Ida May Park. They cast him in roles in which he could utilize his talent for characterization. The star of most of the films was Dorothy Phillips, stage actress, who was one of Universal's most popular players. Although Chaney had no real hopes of becoming a big star, he was sure he had a solid future as a character actor. Not only was this an artistic consideration but a practical one: as he himself explained later, he could always work character parts no matter how old he became and he was not the leading man type. Since he was able to command such mobility of features even without make-up, he could play a variety

Lon Chaney and Dorothy Phillips in an early Universal film in which the signs of aging are indicated by the greying hair at the temples.

of character roles. Chaney was particularly successful as the villain, like Sleter Noble in *Hell Morgan's Girl,* a 1917 film set in San Francisco's Barbary Coast.

It is almost impossible to determine exactly at what point the direction of Chaney's career began to change. Perhaps it was with his second marriage. Perhaps it was in 1915 when Universal City opened one of the largest operations in the industry, giving him the opportunity to appear in bigger and better parts, yet, because of the bigness of the operation, keeping him in a relatively minor position. Chaney was completely absorbed in his work and apparently did not assess his own worth in terms of popularity or money. His salary had increased to sixty and then finally seventy-five dollars a week, which was small compared to what some film players were earning, but adequate to him. He may not have realized he was giving so much for so little.

At the urging of his wife, who understood and recognized his talents, and was evidently more aware than he of what was happening in the industry, he asked for an additional fifty dollars and a five-year contract. The studio manager, William Sistrom, told him he was just another actor and would never be worth over one hundred a week. It was a rebuff Chaney would never forget and in later years always showed this quirk by demanding an extra fifty dollars a week when offered a contract by any studio, whatever the salary. He left Universal. Years later he returned, not as just another actor, but as a star, to make two motion picture classics. His apprenticeship was over.

Free-Lance Journeyman

During the next six years, Chaney appeared in over thirty films, playing a variety of roles including Western heavies, gangsters, Chinese, fur trappers, pirates, some good and some evil. But it was his excellent portrayals in character parts of a more unusual nature that put him in a unique position. As he established a reputation and a following, the law of supply and demand worked in his favor. The audiences wanted to see more of him so the studios used him in stories in which his particular talents could be exploited. He created a niche for himself.

There was great movement in the motion picture industry, with many independent producing companies fighting for survival as the major producers got bigger, and players moved from one studio to another. Chaney was not unknown, but the competition was very keen. After making the rounds of the other studios, including Fox, Goldwyn, and Triangle, without success, he almost considered returning to Universal. However, the Fates were again at work. William S. Hart, the screen's greatest Western actor, and one of the most highly paid, had recently severed connections with Triangle and signed with Paramount, where he was preparing a picture for production. Hart had seen Chaney do a heavy role in one of the Universal films and liked his work, so Lon was summoned to the studio and interviewed by the studio manager and by the director, Lambert

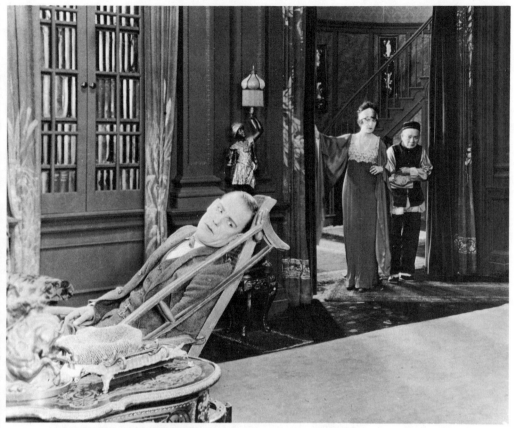

In this 1923 film, **The Shock,** Chaney used crutches in creating his role of the crippled messenger of a gang leader.

Hillyer. Both told Chaney he was too short to play opposite Hart, who was over six feet tall, but Hart insisted this was no obstacle, since Chaney was a good actor. The first attempts to do a scene together were not successful, but when Hart suggested they switch roles for the moment, Chaney understood better the effect that was desired. He excused himself and asked if they could do the scene later in the day, explaining that this was the first time he had done a scene with a star of Hart's prominence. As it turned out, Hart's judgment and faith in him was justified for Chaney turned in a strong performance in *Riddle Gawne*, opening the way to other opportunities.

During this period Lon Chaney worked for a number of studios in a variety of roles that allowed him to use his knowledge of

The French Canadian trapper in **The Trap** was a specific regional type. Since he was the leading man, the only make-up he used was a wig. The wavy hair helped to soften the face and create a more sympathetic expression. The story, by Chaney and Irving Thalberg, covered a span of time that required the characters to age.

make-up to great advantage. They served to establish his reputation, not only as a fine actor, but as the foremost portrayer of grotesque characters. He drew on his knowledge of make-up, his observation of people, and his imagination to create his roles. Make-up was only part of the character. Chaney never relied entirely on the visual effect but used it only as the framework within which the character existed. He considered the mental and emotional aspects as well to give credence and depth to the whole.

Since many films were being made from novels and plays, he drew upon the author's creations, although some of the adaptations did not always follow the original story line. Anyone who has read *Notre Dame de Paris* can recognize how faithfully he interpreted Victor Hugo's hunchback.

Scene from **Danger—Go Slow** (1918) with Lon Chaney and Mae Murray. The director was Robert Z. Leonard with whom Chaney had worked on the stage.

Spottiswood Aitkin, Priscilla Dean, and Lon Chaney in a scene from **The Wicked Darling**. This 1919 film was Chaney's first association with director Tod Browning. Browning worked at Universal Studios from 1918 to 1923 writing and directing a number of films with Universal's star player, Priscilla Dean, who had made her reputation playing a crook. Chaney, too, played many gangster roles, which almost type-cast him.

The make-up created by Chaney was the result of intense study on his part. The standard stereotypes of the stage were no longer adequate for a discerning audience, nor were they satisfactory for the creative artist. He said in an interview that he would often go to different sections of the city to observe the characteristics of people of various nationalities in order to more faithfully recreate life. One can imagine this unassuming man in his favorite street dress of old grey coat with turned up collar, cap pulled over his forehead, and heavy rimmed glasses, moving about unrecognized, absorbing the movements and characteristics of the people who served as proto-

Lon Chaney, Wheeler Oakman, and Priscilla Dean in Tod Browning's 1921 Universal film **Outside the Law.** In a dual role, Chaney was billed as "Guess Who" for the Oriental Joe Wang. This was his second appearance in a Browning picture.

types for his screen creations. One of the reasons for his great popularity was his ability to inject into his characters a sense of reality even when the original role suggested no such depth. Attention to detail, however small, is essential to any characterization. The audiences were not always aware that behind the screen image they viewed was a consummate actor.

When George Loane Tucker was casting *The Miracle Man* at Paramount he considered using a contortionist for the part of Frog, the fake cripple. Chaney was able to make an appointment to try out for the part. He said that when he went home later to think out how to play Frog he noticed that while sitting in his chair he had crossed his legs and unconsciously tucked his right foot behind his left ankle as he sometimes had a habit of doing. This gave him the

As Mark Shore in **All the Brothers Were Valiant.**

idea of emphasizing his twisted legs in this tortuous-looking position to heighten the effect of a dramatic "healing" scene. He then worked out his conception of the character, had his audition and was hired. The picture was very successful and established Chaney as an actor;

as well as furthering the careers of Thomas Meighan and Betty Compson. Chaney's startling physical performance did not overshadow his sensitive handling of the other facets of his role. For his performance he was paid one hundred and twenty-five dollars a week, a little more than was predicted for his chances at Universal. For a later performance in *The Penalty* he asked for and got five hundred.

Not all of the movies being turned out were made without regard for the artistic nature of the media. Many directors strove to create something of a more lasting nature, utilizing photography, lighting,

Ben Deely, Wallace Beery, and Lon Chaney in the first filming of a Joseph Conrad novel, **Victory,** directed by Maurice Tourneur and released in 1919. Although Chaney often helped other actors with their make-up, Beery's beard, though imaginative, lacks Chaney's realistic touch.

Study of a pirate. The evil look, indicated by the straggly hair and whiskers and bushy eyebrows, is accented by the elongated putty nose.

In **The Penalty,** a hat manufacturing company was the front behind which Blizzard conducted his criminal activities as king of the underworld. Because a childhood operation by a supposedly careless surgeon lost him his legs, he swore revenge on society and the surgeon. Chaney showed the overwhelming anger and hatred the character possessed in his mobile face.

settings, stories, acting, editing to create what they wanted. Maurice Tourneur was one of them.

Tourneur's film of Joseph Conrad's *Victory* included another of Chaney's villainous portraits, that of the pock-marked Ricardo. The picture had good reviews despite some distortion of the story line. Liberties were again taken with *Treasure Island* in which Chaney played two roles, the blind pirate Pew and the pirate Merry. Shirley Mason was cast as the young boy Jim Hawkins. The next picture Chaney made with Tourneur was *The Glory of Love,* which was filmed in 1920 but not released until 1923 under the title *While Paris*

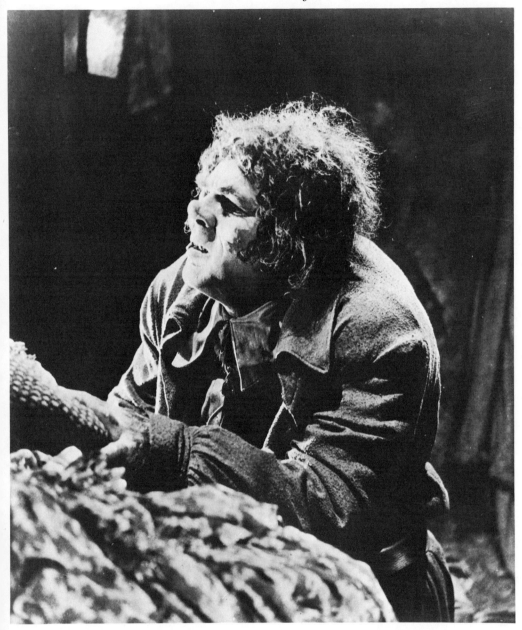

Sleeps. It was a forerunner of the wax museum, mad scientist epics of a later day.

Each of Chaney's roles during this period brought him closer to his most memorable creation. He made a giant step in *The Penalty*,

a picture in which he demonstrated his willingness, perhaps his
desire, to put himself through torture for the sake of realism. A
lesser performer would have taken advantage of lighting and camera
angles to achieve much of the effect of a legless man. Instead, he
devised a harness that strapped his lower legs back against his

thighs and walked with heavy leather stumps on his knees. The shock value of his appearance nearly overshadowed his skill as an actor.

Two roles during this period, the Chinese laundryman in *Shadows* and Fagin in *Oliver Twist*, were highly praised by the eminent critic Robert E. Sherwood.

As the portrayer of the physically deformed, he was now to appear in the role that epitomized all that Lon Chaney was and was to become. The character the author created was given life and substance by Chaney's skill. Every bit of knowledge of acting, of make-up, and picture-making technique, of personal heartache and suffering of the man, were fused together in the characterization. The agility with which he moved about belied the torture he suffered under the pounds of hump, frontal protuberance, and hairy skin-like rubber that covered the harness he wore to bend his body into that of a hunchback. The ingenious and heavy facial make-up added to his discomfort. He was able to work only for short periods of time before the cameras, because of the pain and because his perspiration would ruin the make-up.

The high-budget *Hunchback of Notre Dame* had taken three months to do at a cost of over a million dollars. When released in September of 1923, it was immediately successful, in time grossing well over its cost. Lon Chaney had given a journeyman performance at the studio of his apprenticeship, where one executive had told him he was merely another actor. He was now truly a star.

The Star

O ut of the tremendous activities of the mid-twenties emerged a combination of talent and enterprise that became Metro-Goldwyn-Mayer. It was called the Home of the Stars, but by no means housed all of the stars, for all the major studios boasted bright names. It was a time of bigness: the stars were bigger, the productions were bigger. There was something for everybody: bath-tub to Bible, comedy to cavalcade, sin, salvation, sex and censorship, adventure, romance, spectacle, and even art.

When M-G-M was formed, Irving Thalberg moved from Universal to become production chief. It was Thalberg who had supervised *The Hunchback of Notre Dame* and had recognized the potential of the actor he had chosen for the role. There is an interesting story concerning Chaney's salary for that film. An unnamed studio official who first contacted Chaney, laughed at his price of $1,500 a week. The studio couldn't get anyone else, so Chaney was again contacted and this time asked for $2,000 a week. Again a refusal. But still no one else for the part, so back to the telephone went the official. This time the salary was raised to $2,500, and Chaney advised the official that every time he called the salary demand would be raised another $500. Chaney's salary was $2,500 a week.

Thalberg convinced Chaney to sign a one year contract with the newly formed studio. It was to be a profitable venture for both as

Chaney's pictures made money and gave him the opportunity to create some extraordinary roles. It should be recognized that any tightly organized unit in the business of making money must follow a certain formula and impose limitations on its various elements. It was fortunate that a man like Thalberg was in charge of production because he had an innate sense of making commercial successes that still had artistic integrity. And he was not afraid to spend big money in re-shooting *Ben Hur* or changing directors in *The Merry Widow*.

It is difficult to assess whether Lon Chaney's films during this period enhanced or hampered his own artistic growth. He certainly was successful and the roles he created could not have been done by anyone else with the same effectiveness. In spite of his reputation as the exponent of bizarre and grotesque roles, he achieved critical acclaim when he was required to project his ability as an actor rather than hide behind make-up. It is unfortunate that his fame rested so much on his shock roles. In a sense it is a great compliment to his expertness that he was able to seem something other than what he really was.

That he is remembered as a horror actor is unfair. Only a few of his roles could be classed as horror, in the sense that the characters existed almost beyond the limits of plausibility. The ape man in *The Blind Bargain* was the result of experiments with animals; the vampire in *London After Midnight* was a deus ex machina. Both Quasimodo and Eric were deformed by nature at birth. His make-up disguises were the forerunners of the present-day monsters, but the interpretations, particularly of the latter two, had more substance and motivation than any of the remakes or subsequent films in the genre. It would be interesting but ineffectual to speculate what Chaney would have done with the sound version of *Frankenstein* or *Dracula* for which he was slated.

Chaney probably did not choose his roles himself. He was quoted as saying he didn't seek out stories, that was the job of the studio. Though he apparently did not rebel at any of his roles and was not temperamental (and wouldn't tolerate any inclination toward temperament in his co-workers), he was a good workman even if not always tractable. He was cooperative while working but insisted on his rights. When Thalberg asked him to work overtime to finish some scenes because otherwise the extras and stage hands would have to be called for an extra day, Chaney said his working day ended at five o'clock, he always had dinner at six-thirty, he wasn't too concerned with the costs, and anyway the set workers could use an extra day's pay. This victory may not have set well with the executives but certainly endeared him to the stagehands and extras. He apparently had no desire to associate with the executives except on a business level and seemed more at ease with the technicians.

Although this perhaps apocryphal account best serves to illustrate his sense of independence and his protection of his hard-won rights, he was not unmindful of the production problems of the studio. If he sometimes helped the stage hands shift scenery on his set, it was because he identified with them; and if he halted production when one of them was hurt, it was because he was concerned. It was said his contract contained a clause requiring him to make up time lost by illness in order to maintain the production schedules.

His private life was his own; he said, "between pictures there is no Lon Chaney." He did not like interviews and did not participate in the Hollywood social whirl, appearing in public only when necessary. He had a small, close circle of friends, some of whom were not in the movie world. For relaxation he spent time in the mountains, fishing and photographing wild-life. Photography was one of his main interests; and he was the subject of an article in *The American Cinematographer*. His love of the outdoors no doubt stemmed from his early years in Colorado, but he used it as an escape from the arduous schedules of picture making.

The desire to have no intrusion into his private life helped the studios create the publicity enforced image of the man of mystery. Yet he was relatively a simple man who had no pretensions and apparently exhibited none of the signs of the affectations generally associated with stars. He worked hard, was proud of his achievements, and respected craftsmanship. There is no doubt he maintained a high degree of self-discipline and expected it in others. When he saw younger players working seriously, he would spend hours of his busy day helping them with their lines.

On his last day on the M-G-M set, after completing what was to be his last film, *The Unholy Three*, he asked that a picture be taken of him and the entire crew and that the copies be distributed among them. This simple gesture expressing his appreciation and saying farewell without sentimentality was an example of his reticence to reveal personal feelings. He was uneasy and gruff when offered thanks or profusive congratulations.

Studio publicity and the various interviews and true life stories

Chaney as the scientist in the early sequences of **He Who Gets Slapped,** his first contract film as a star of the newly-formed studio combining Metro, Goldwyn, and Mayer. The moustache and goatee are that of a pre-revolutionary Russian aristocrat.

that appeared constantly were obviously designed to create a public image without stating too many facts. However, the isolated bits and pieces tend to fill out the skeleton and indicate, if not the whole, at least the essence. Of the offscreen man it was said by various chroniclers that he was worth about $2 million, owned three automobiles, was an authority on penology and had been made honorary member of police departments of several cities. His personal appearances at filmland functions were extremely rare, and his street dress was such that he was unrecognizable. Whatever aid he gave others was a private matter, though indications are that he assisted many. By the time he reached stardom he was in a position to help those who had helped him and those who were struggling as he had.

Norma Shearer, John Gilbert, and Lon Chaney in their circus costumes. The make-up and costume is that of the traditional clown.

The first picture made under the trademark of the newly formed M-G-M studio was *He Who Gets Slapped*, a play by Andreyev that had been performed on Broadway two years before with Richard Bennett in the lead role. It was a prestige picture with Chaney in the title part. Viktor Sjöström, the Swedish director, adapted the play and produced a beautifully photographed and moving film. Some reviewers said Chaney did the best work of his career, performing with breadth, force and imagination. Two of the other players in this picture, John Gilbert and Norma Shearer, became tremendously popular in the ensuing years.

Chaney's next vehicle was Crane Wilbur's play *The Monster*, which gave him the opportunity to portray an almost tongue-in-cheek version of the mad doctor in *The Blind Bargain*. The film was a thriller, not without its comic relief, and shows the type of character most audiences would pay to see him play.

The same year, 1925, Tod Browning, who had directed Chaney in some previous Universal films, approached Thalberg with an unusual story that seemed a good Chaney vehicle, Clarence Robbins's 1917 novel *The Unholy Three*. The combination of an imaginative director, a perceptive producer, and a creative actor resulted in a film that grossed well over $2 million and was the beginning of a collaboration that was to produce major personal and financial successes. The subsequent Browning-Chaney films gave the actor opportunity to portray those grotesque characters that challenged his ability and imagination, and thrilled his audiences. Browning wrote most of the stories.

Thalberg was careful to use Chaney's talents well. The bizarre

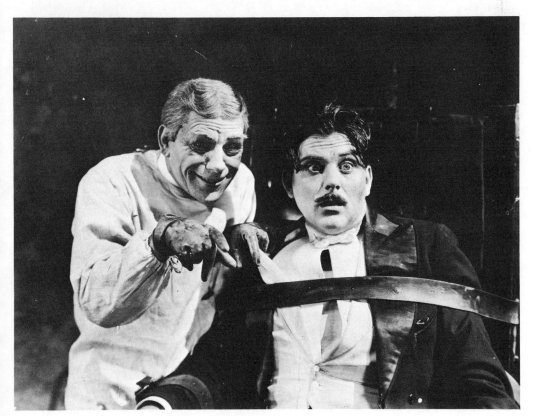

Chaney and Hallam Cooley in **The Monster**.

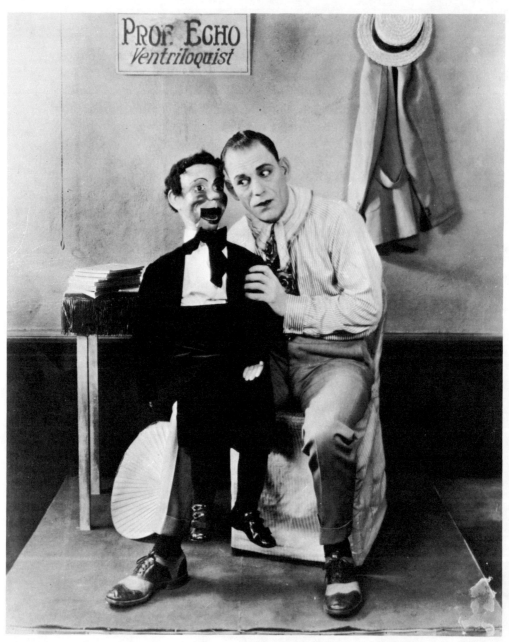

Chaney as the sideshow ventriloquist in **The Unholy Three.**

roles were balanced with good character parts. The strategy behind
varying the roles was to keep Chaney on top by not giving the
audiences too much of the same thing at once. Each new Chaney
film was eagerly awaited by his fans and the studio publicity piqued

their curiosity, for no one was sure what his latest make-up would be. Even in the films in which he played straight roles there was always the possibility he might appear in a minor character role, unbilled. His screen image was such that he became the target of a joke, attributed to Marshall Neilan, the director, "Don't step on it, it may be Lon Chaney."

In September of 1925, Universal's *The Phantom of the Opera* was finally released. Shooting had started in late 1924 and a first version was previewed in January 1925. It had taken about ten weeks to do, although another eight months were spent in re-shooting some scenes, which were deleted in the final version. The picture was an immediate success and Chaney's make-up was as startling as in *The Hunchback*. There was much publicity but no advance photos of him were made available. The suspense was heightened by the fact that his face was not revealed to the audience until midway in the film when the heroine snatches the mask from his face in one of the most terrifying scenes in any Chaney picture.

The last Chaney picture released in 1925 was *The Tower of Lies*. Viktor Sjöström used Selma Lagerlof's novel *The Emperor of Portugallia* as the basis for his somber and symbolic film. One reviewer called it "one of the most beautiful and poetic of photoplays." Chaney gives a remarkable portrayal of the old Swedish peasant who, grief-crazed when his daughter leaves to go to the city, imagines himself the medieval emperor of her childhood games. The film was never widely acclaimed, perhaps because of its subtlety and artistry.

During the next four years seven of the thirteen films Chaney made were directed by Tod Browning. The combination proved successful at the box-office and made Chaney one of Hollywood's most popular stars. The two worked out a series of bizarre and startling films that enabled Chaney to create the make-up effects that earned him the title of "The Man of a Thousand Faces." He had to use what would now be regarded as primitive means. He never wore a mask and his effects were achieved primarily by use of the materials which were a carry-over from the stage: grease paint, putty, mortician's wax, gutta percha, fishskin, lining pencils, crepe hair, and collodion. Refinements such as latex rubber and the synthetics, to say nothing of liquid make-ups and superior photographic technique came much later. In the essay Lon Chaney wrote for *The Encyclopaedia Britannica* he describes some methods for applying make-up, but it is said many of his secrets died with him. The procedures described by

The old peasant and his daughter (Norma Shearer).

Cecil Holland, head of M-G-M's make-up department, in his book *The Art of Make-Up for Stage and Screen,* for which Chaney wrote the preface, are remarkably similar to those in Chaney's article.

The six years at M-G-M as a big star were most certainly reward-ing to Lon Chaney, as he was not only successful in his career but also financially secure. If it now appeared that his roles were less taxing physically, it was not because he applied himself any less to them. It was his skill that made them seem easy. One of his most difficult parts was in *The Blackbird,* which was released early in 1926. Playing two characters, one of whom was a man whose entire side was paralyzed, he had to keep his joints and muscles rigid while working for hours in front of the cameras. Any slight move-ment would have necessitated retakes. This movie was a kind of twist on the Dr. Jekyll and Mr. Hyde theme, the straight man being evil and the crooked man good. In most of the Browning-Chaney

West End Bertie (Owen Moore) and the Blackbird (Chaney).

Bertie and the Bishop.

Walthall, Nagel, and Chaney.

films the plot evolved from the characterization, for Browning's idea was to have the audience believe the horrible possible, not impossible, thus increasing the terror.

Another film started with the idea of an armless man. In *The Unknown*, Chaney had his arms strapped tightly to his body, demonstrating again what discomfort he would undergo to create a character. In this film, Chaney played an armless knife-thrower who would, for the love of a girl, have his arms amputated.

In the other pictures Chaney appeared as a man with one blind eye; the dual role of a Scotland Yard inspector and a vampire with make-up as startling as that of the Phantom; a big city gangster (straight); and a wild animal hunter whose face had been ravaged with claw marks. One film Browning directed, but did not write, was taken from the Broadway play *Kongo*, starring Walter Huston. The photoplay was titled *West of Zanzibar*, and Chaney appeared as a man whose legs were paralyzed.

James Murray, Marcelline Day, and Lon Chaney.

In *Tell It to the Marines* he gave one of his best performances, in a straight, no make-up role, depicting a tough, but human, Marine sergeant. He was so good that the character became the prototype for the innumerable service films that followed. In roles such as this, as well as the detective in *While the City Sleeps*, and the railroad engineer in *Thunder*, he did not impersonate the character but became the person, bringing a realism to the parts that gained the respect of the people in the professions portrayed.

His regard for accuracy led him to the studies of anatomy and physiognomy; this, coupled with his ability for acute observation of people, gave to his creations more than the mere illusion of authenticity. He was not content to use mere convention; such as accenting the angle of the eye to play an oriental. He examined the structure of the cheekbones, nose, lips, eyes, as well as the bodily movements

Lon Chaney and Lupe Velez in **Where East Is East.**

In one segment of **West of Zanzibar** the cripple used a small wheeled platform for locomotion.

William Haines and Lon Chaney.

Eleanor Boardman and Lon Chaney.

Barbara Bedford and Chaney.

Chaney and Bernard Seigel.

to establish the whole character. He played many Orientals in films, including *Outside the Law, Bits of Life,* and an outstanding portrayal of the Chinese laundryman in *Shadows,* which Robert Sherwood called the finest interpretation of an Oriental by an Occidental he had ever seen. Chaney's three ages of *Mr. Wu* was even more remarkable, for he played three distinct generations: grandfather, father and son.

Chaney was a dull-witted peasant in *Mockery,* a film written and directed by Benjamin Christensen, the Danish director-actor of the somber Scandinavian school. Chaney created a make-up and characterization appropriate to revolutionary Russia, but the film was not particularly distinguished.

A favorite theme of actors and audiences is the broken-hearted clown. If the role is good an actor can run the entire emotional gamut, while the audience indulges itself in tears and laughter. *Laugh, Clown, Laugh,* which Chaney called his favorite film, gave him such a part. Taken from the stage play starring Lionel Barrymore, it was a fine film, directed by Herbert Brenon and photographed by James Wong Howe. Chaney's clown face appeared on the cover of the sheet music of the hit title song. The heroine was fifteen-year-old Loretta Young.

In 1927 sound hit the movies with a deafening roar; theatre audiences began to dwindle and so did receipts. A public so faithful to silent movies turned its attention to the sound of radio. And while the studios decided which of the sound systems to use and whether to convert completely to talking pictures, more and more people stayed away from the theatres. The studios still turned out good and successful silents but were reshooting some scenes with dubbed in dialogue and issuing some with sound scores. The production companies were in a perilous position: the tremendous outlay for sound equipment, both in the studios and in the theatres, and the lesser box-office receipts caused layoffs and cutbacks.

During the transition period, Chaney's silent films continued to be successes. In 1928, the year of M-G-M's first all-talking picture *The Broadway Melody,* he was the most popular actor in the movies, and Clara Bow the most popular actress. But interest began to lag somewhat in his films and in 1929 only two were released; but then that year was not a very good one for anyone.

The last silent film he made was *Thunder,* in which he portrayed a crusty, old railroad engineer. Some of the studio publicity said he actually drove the engine. During the filming he became ill, developing pneumonia, but finished the picture. He later had several operations to correct a throat ailment, which was said to have been aggravated by a piece of false snow which had lodged in his throat during the filming.

There was much speculation about his making talking pictures: as some said that he was hesitant because he felt they might destroy pantomime, that the public might not receive him as well, and of course the inevitable rumors that he could not talk because his parents had been mute. One of the prime reasons for his delay in making talkies was that he was negotiating a new contract for a reported $5,000 a week.

But he could talk and talk he did, in five different voices as the ventriloquist in the remake of his earlier success *The Unholy Three.* He consulted voice coaches who assured him his voice would record

Scene from **Thunder.**

well. During this time he was a sick man, though he was unaware how seriously ill he was. It seemed that the years of self-inflicted punishment, hard work, and dedication to work began to tell on him so that when he became ill he simply did not have enough strength to fight it.

The Unholy Three was a great success and assured his future career in talking pictures. A number of films were in prospect: *The Sea Bat, The Bugle Sounds, Cheri Bibi,* and *Dracula.* Unfortunately a month after the release of his first talking picture, Lon Chaney died of throat cancer.

Chaney's illness began while he was filming *Thunder,* his last silent movie. He developed pneumonia after filming some snow scenes in Wisconsin. His tonsils were removed to alleviate an aggravated throat condition.

After release of that film he was busy negotiating a new contract,

Harry Earles and Lon Chaney in **The Unholy Three.**

Chaney and Lila Lee.

Lila Lee, Elliott Nugent, and Lon Chaney.

preparing for his first talking picture, and trying to rest to regain his strength.

Upon completion of *The Unholy Three* he went to New York to consult with medical specialists and then retired to his cabin in the High Sierras. Doctors knew his months were numbered because of cancer. A hemorrhage, brought on by a state of anemia, sent him to St. Vincent's Hospital in Los Angeles on Wednesday, August 20th. He was given blood transfusions. A third transfusion was given the following Saturday and his condition pronounced critical. Attendants were confident he was improving, but he suffered another throat hemorrhage and within half an hour Lon Chaney died at 12:55 the morning of Tuesday, August 26, 1930.

The funeral services the following Thursday were attended by notables of the film colony and by many of the people whom Chaney had befriended and known. The musicians who had played mood music on the set while he was filming played some of his favorite music, especially the song "Laugh, Clown, Laugh."

A poignant tribute was given to Chaney at the Hollywood American Legion Stadium where he regularly attended the boxing bouts on Friday nights. The announcer stepped into the ring and called attention to the vacant seat which Chaney had always occupied. The lights went out and Alan Hale, the actor, with a flashlight illuminating his face, read a poem in Chaney's memory. A reporter, describing the audience's response, said it "was a touching tribute from men to the memory of a man's man."

All M-G-M workers throughout the world ceased work for five minutes when the salute was fired by representatives of the United States Marine Corps at the funeral. A eulogy was delivered by Lieutenant Colonel H. S. Dyar, Marine Corps chaplain.

Chaney was reported to be conservatively worth a million and a half dollars. His will disposed of property valued at $550,000, the bulk going to his widow. His first wife received no legacy. His son had been previously provided for. His brothers and sister had been provided for by his life insurance. The sum of $5000 was left to John Jeske, his chauffeur and valet, "faithful friend and at all times a loyal and faithful servant."

Hazel Chaney survived her husband by several years. An obituary notice stated that Frances Cleveland Bush (Cleva Creighton) died November 21, 1967, of a stroke in a Sierra Madre, California, convalescent home at the age of 78.

After so many years since Lon Chaney's passing there are many who remember him as the greatest of all time. He was a fine artist, not merely the progenitor of a series of inadequate and sometimes impossible horror films. There was no real successor to Chaney. Those actors who appeared in these later films were limited by their own personalities and could not create a total character themselves. They had to be put into a series of masks created by the make-up men. When the screen biography of Lon Chaney, *The Man of a Thousand Faces,* was made in 1957, with James Cagney in the title role, the recreations of Chaney's make-ups, remarkable in themselves, were but pale imitations of the real thing.

Film Roles

L on Chaney's film roles were for the most part received favor-
ably by critics and audiences. After six years of hard work he
came into real prominence with *The Miracle Man*. The picture
itself was an important one, and the *New York Times* termed it and
Griffith's *Broken Blossoms* the two most important works of the year.
It was from this point that Chaney moved to stardom.

The story concerned a quartet of crooks who saw an opportunity
to capitalize on a faith healer, an old blind man known as the
Patriarch. Chaney played one of the crooks who twisted his body
into a pathetic shape and dragged himself along the city streets
begging for money and stealing when the opportunity arose. The
plan was for Chaney to be miraculously "healed" by the Patriarch
to lure the "suckers" to contribute to the cause of faith. The plan
backfired when the goodness and faith of the Miracle Man enveloped
each of the crooks. Chaney really played two completely different
characters: the one physical, the other emotional. Each was consis-
tent in itself. This was a trait he demonstrated in all his acting
chores. The character he created was complete and did not vary.
When he was the larcenous fake he was mean and dirty, insulting
and contemptuous of the law and people. His personality suited his
feigned twisted body. After his reformation he became a warm and
loving person, which he conveyed by his facial expressions and ges-

Betty Compson, Thomas Meighan, Joseph Dowling, J. M. Dumont, and Lon Chaney in **The Miracle Man.** This was an important and difficult film for Chaney. His role required him to project the change of personality from a mean and bitter to a warm and loving person. He proved to be an actor of great sensitivity. This 1919 film gave him the direction he needed to find success.

tures without becoming ineffectual. The role showed the range of his ability and gave his acting a new dimension.

Of several films made after *The Miracle Man* the *New York Times* commented:

Victory
No screen actor whose name comes to mind can equal Mr.

Chaney in the impersonation of intense, strongly marked types. He does with consummate skill and fine finish the kind of acting that many attempt with lumbering ponderosity and maladroit exaggeration.

Treasure Island
The most vivid acting is done by the dependable Lon Chaney in two roles, first, as the blind Pew, and then as the surly Merry.

Nomads of the North
The actors in the picture are suited to its story. All of them at times overdo their parts, especially Betty Blythe and Lon Chaney in the leading roles, but these two, and the others, make amends for their strained and heavy scenes by sure and vivid acting in others.

The Penalty was another example of Chaney's forceful projection. Here as in *The Miracle Man* his appearance was a shock—a legless man moving about on his stumps. But as the audience became more absorbed in the strength of his presence on the screen his condition intruded less and less. The actor commanded the attention.

The story was weak and contrived, about a man who had had his legs needlessly amputated years before and who swore revenge on the surgeon. He became the ruler of the underworld, planning to loot a government bank. A hat factory was his front. He contrives a meeting with, and poses for, the daughter of the surgeon, a sculptress doing a bust of Satan. He wants to have new legs grafted onto his stumps and machinations to achieve this are complicated. She will be held as hostage and the legs of her fiance will be used for the operation. The surgeon instead removes a brain tumor which also removes his motivations.

The cinematic version was probably the best that could have been done with the novel. In spite of his tortured mental state before the operation, the arch-criminal cannot bring himself to destroy the girl who manipulates the pedals of the piano he plays so beautifully even though he knows she is a government spy. After the operation he is killed by a former henchman. This is certainly more realistic and dramatic than the novel in which he is reformed, marries the girl who helped him at the piano, and becomes a philanthropic force in the community. Obviously the penalty for an evil life should be paid.

In spite of the sometimes inadequate story, Chaney did more with the role than required for a film that may have served only as a

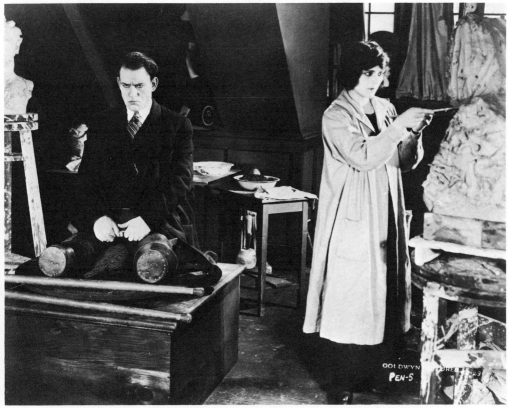

The sculptress (Claire Adams), seeing "wickedness but also awe and wonder" and the "tortured look" of a fallen angel on the face of the legless man, induces him to pose for her bust of Satan **(The Penalty)**.

showcase for his particular talent for the grotesque. He enlivened his character with emotion. The expressions of rage and hatred, and of sensitivity, especially when he played the piano, drew the audience's attention away from the physical.

This role was a preparation for the Hunchback, still in the future. Chaney and director William Worsley began a rapport that developed with *The Blind Bargain* and culminated with *The Hunchback of Notre Dame*.

THE HUNCHBACK OF NOTRE DAME

The magnificence of this production with its faithful recreation

of 15th-century Paris, and particularly of the famous cathedral, almost made the actors seem insignificant. But as the attention focused
on the people, one character became the center of the story, a
catalyst, in effect.

Quasimodo, the bell-ringer, was a concentration of all the parts of
man and society. He touched all of the characters in some way and
he was part of the city and the church. As the story unfolded new
facets were revealed. He, too, had his own personality.

In the film, Quasimodo looked as if he had stepped from the pages
of the book. Chaney's recreation was absolute. It was difficult to
realize that it was an actor playing a part. When he is seen high up
on the cathedral, taunting and jeering at the crowd below, and
clambering about the parapets, he seems a part of the building,
a gargoyle come alive.

Chaney's portrayal is his own classic one, as well as the classic interpretation of the role. If audiences came away with feelings of sympathy and admiration for the hunchback it was due more to Chaney's projection than to the character of the story. From behind that rigid make-up, which took him four hours to apply, he was able to express loyalty, devotion, hate, tenderness, and disappointment, without seeming to make ludicrous grimaces.

The role of Quasimodo is a ready-made dramatic one, if taken only as a part of a sweeping play. It could be played simply as a dumb, lumbering monstrosity of a man, serving only as a foil for the other characters. Chaney drew a carefully examined portrait with defined and logical motives. It was not a character that was moved along by the other characters, but one that reacted to them and made his own moves. He developed as the film proceeded.

There was unquestioned loyalty to his master until he had to

Gladys Brockwell, Chaney, and Patsy Ruth Miller.

defend the girl against his master's evil, until then not understood. His devotion to the girl who had taken pity on him maintained even through his disappointment of knowing she loved another. His hatred was immense when he threw stones and timbers, and poured hot metal on the rabble he thought had come to harm the girl he regarded with such tenderness.

Chaney's remarkable performance has sustained not only as an example of his creativity in make-up and characterization but of his pantomimic art as well.

THE PHANTOM OF THE OPERA

Erik, the Phantom, is a creature who elicits little admiration. Besides the chill of terror, in Chaney's hands he has moments of sympathy, particularly when it is realized that in his curious, fiendish way, he has a passion for the woman as well as her voice. To over-emphasize that aspect of the role would have destroyed the effectiveness of the presentation and would have made the Phantom much less frightening.

Chaney moved through his scenes with the swiftness and ethereal quality of the fantasy he portrayed and lent to his characterization that element of bizarre terror that the role and story called for. He was a real part of the seemingly unreal subterranean domain.

His disguise was so perfect that he was totally unidentifiable as Lon Chaney. The only clues to his identity were the unmistakable use of his expressive hands and the movements of his body. Many of his gestures and postures were exaggerated but only to the extent they were in keeping with the macabre settings in which he was placed.

The role of the Phantom, like that of Quasimodo, was particularly suited to his talents. To achieve the visual appearance required ingenious use of make-up. To provide motivation and action that was logical required study of the character and his background. There were indications that there was disagreement between Chaney and the director, Rupert Julian. These disagreements no doubt were based on interpretation. Chaney, in his desire to create a total character, did not want to subordinate his character to the sets and photography, which were very impressive.

Scene of the Red Death.

The film is still an effective one, even when viewed by today's more sophisticated audience. It tells its story and presents its characters as it was intended. The unmasking scene is still as dramatic as it was when first shown. Erik's dismay and anger at the young woman's curiosity is much like Lohengrin's disappointment at Elsa's persistence in learning his identity. This act of distrust speeds up the fateful outcome.

Throughout the film Erik was a symbol of terror and defiance. Chaney sustained this image till the closing scene. After a hectic chase through the Paris streets Erik is at the river's edge, the mob closing in on him. He raises his hand high above his head. The crowd, thinking he holds a grenade, falls back. Then Erik, in a magnificent final gesture of defiance, slowly opens his empty hand and laughs hideously. The mob closes in on him.

When Chaney was star at M-G-M, his roles were less developmental, in the sense of one preparing him for the next, as they were exercises in versatility. Each was a separate effort, approached with professionalism. He had become a much better actor than he was given credit for. His association with grotesque parts kept alive the image of the man of a thousand faces, but in other films he showed he could be effective without make-up.

After his death the studio announced that Wallace Beery was to be his successor. At first glance this seems incongruous considering Mr. Beery's subsequent successes. On closer examination it is apparent that Chaney could have played many with equal success. There was evidence of humor in some of his films. There was evidence of a more subtle approach to characterization. The broad playing required in some of the more theatrical pieces was toned down in the more conventional stories. The style of acting required

Erik at the organ after his unmasking by Christine.

Pose as the Phantom.

for silent pictures depended on pantomime and exaggeration. Talking pictures required new techniques.

The talkie version of *The Unholy Three* is a most revealing film. Chaney adapted to the new medium successfully. The sometimes over-played mannerisms and gestures were entirely in keeping with those of a carnival performer. The sound of his voice and his speech were not alien to the character. That he was able to alter the pitch and timbre of his voice suggests innumerable vocal characterizations. There are moments in the film when the color of his voice and his diction take on classical proportions.

Chaney's M-G-M films can be grouped as: the Browning films, in which the Chaney of the thousand faces was emphasized; the art films, in which the picture-making techniques were prominent rather than his portrayal; the in-between films, in which the accent was less on the macabre than on character.

This publicity shot of a drenched Phantom (after his underwater sequence in the film) illustrates how durable and flexible Chaney's make-up was.

There were eight Browning-Chaney films, all but one of which accented the bizarre. That one, *The Big City*, in which he played a crook, was almost light-hearted by comparison. The star and the director had a compatibility, born of previous association in films for another studio and a similarity of background on the stage.

The first was *The Unholy Three* of 1925. The story concerns the alliance of sideshow performers to become jewel thieves, using a pet shop as their base of operations. They are a study in contrasts, among themselves and in themselves. As the story unfolds these contrasts become more apparent. Hercules, the big, strong man is weak inside; Tweedledee, the tiny midget, is cherubic looking but malevolent; Echo, the ventriloquist, is a cautious schemer with a capacity for love. The strong man and the midget commit a murder while robbing a house. The goading midget is killed by the strong

Courtroom scene in **The Unholy Three.**

The Unholy Three (Harry Earles, Victor McLaglan, Lon Chaney).

man, who is killed by the ventriloquist's pet gorilla. Echo loves his young girl accomplice, who loves the young man employed in the pet shop. The young man is accused of the murder. The ventriloquist, by throwing his voice, testifies through the young man in the witness box who is silently mouthing a prayer. He is cleared.

Chaney had the opportunity to bring many facets of characterization into play; as the ventriloquist with his dummy; as the crook planning robberies; disguised as a sweet, old lady; and as a man whose love for a girl leads him to a noble act. Throughout he performed with brilliance and restraint. This was the best, the most natural role of the series.

Most of these pictures were successful at the box-office mainly because of Chaney's appearance. In some the stories were disappointing, but if his performance was not up to his usual standard, his creations were startling. The plots were generally evolved from an idea, either of story twist or of a character. This was somewhat of a limitation but they served as a showcase for Chaney's make-up talents and Browning's directorial and writing skill.

The Blackbird (story by Browning) has Chaney as a Limehouse crook who uses the disguise of a kindly, charitable cripple known as the Bishop for an alibi and hiding place. When the crook becomes the Bishop he is sincerely the man of good will and Chaney plays him that way. The effect is believable, the more so when his alter ego begins to show signs of merging into the good man. Chaney's remarkable ability to project emotional and psychological aspects of a character beyond the physical presentation is again apparent. This quality prevented many of his roles from being unbelievable. A reviewer said of his work "Mr. Chaney's depiction of the two types of the crook is one of the finest exemplifications of screen artistry one would hope to behold."

The Road to Mandalay was a disappointment but not of course to Chaney fans. He came through with another noteworthy make-up achievement, a blind eye. Perhaps the film followed too closely on the heels of *The Blackbird* and was hastily conceived in order to capitalize on its success.

In *The Unknown* Chaney was much more effective. The story was grim, about an apparent armless knife-thrower in love with the daughter of the owner of a Spanish circus. She has a dislike for men's arms about her and seems to be fond of Alonzo. He mistakes this for love. One night when his arms are unstrapped he strangles Estrellita's father after having been given a terrible beating by him.

Chaney in the straight role of the Blackbird.

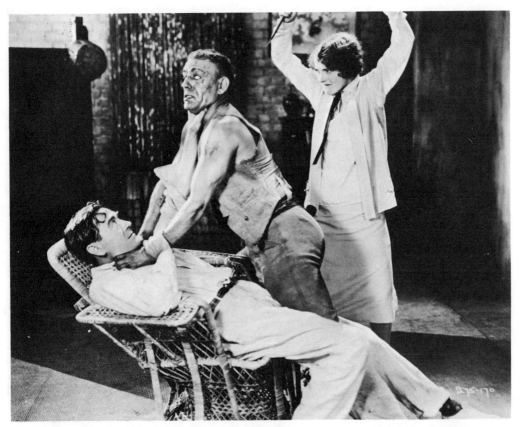

Owen Moore, Lon Chaney, and Lois Moran in a dramatic scene from **The Road to Mandalay** in which the young girl stabs the man attacking her lover, not knowing he is her father.

The only clue to the murderer is that he has a double thumb. Alonzo goes away for an operation, one assumes to have the extra thumb removed, but to have his arms amputated. The plot dictates that course. He is afraid he will be discovered as the murderer and he wishes to marry Estrellita, who hates arms. On his return to the circus he finds her married to Malabar, the strong man, who has shown her there is nothing to fear from arms. Alonzo becomes a man of hate and revenge.

In his act Malabar uses two white horses, one tied to each arm, that run on a treadmill while he attempts to hold them back. Alonzo tries to stop the treadmill so the horses will pull off Malabar's arms,

Alonzo, the Armless Wonder. The wide sash and loose blouse help to create the illusion of a man with no arms. Alonzo threw knives and shot guns with his feet. With this role Chaney became what might be called the total actor: even his feet became part of the characterization.

but the horses are stopped after Alonzo slips and falls beneath the deadly hoofs.

Chaney brought all his acrobatic skills into play for this role. He used his feet as hands when eating, drinking, smoking, and even scratching his head. In one scene he uses his toes to pour out wine even though his arms are free. In another scene his face takes on an expression of malevolent glee as he wiggles his toes in the face of the policeman who is searching for the murderer with a double thumb.

The next two roles that Chaney played in Browning stories were completely opposite ones: one a traditional Scotland Yard detective, all business, restrained and proper; the other an American crook,

Lucille Balfour (Marcelline Day) in the clutches of the vampire as the vampire's daughter (Edna Tichenor) looks on.

crafty but with touches of humor and more lighthearted and flamboyant.

London After Midnight was a murder mystery in which Chaney, as the detective, employs hypnotism to trap the murderer. The gloomy castle, strange figures in the night, and mysterious happenings, all leading to the denouement, were typical of the murder mystery film. Chaney, as the detective, was sure, restrained, and competent, and he stayed within the limitations of a role that gave him little opportunity to extend himself in either characterization or make-up. The introduction of the Vampire added to the atmosphere of mystery and suspense. His make-up was equal to that of the Phantom. When Tod Browning first thought of making *Dracula* he surely envisioned Chaney as both Dracula and Dr. Van Helsing.

The Big City was a contemporary story of crooks cheating crooks. In a no-make-up role Chaney again created a character without resorting to artificial devices. His crook is vain about his clothes, is devious in his scheming, and his motives are more for gain and self-satisfaction than for revenge. He is more of a "good guy."

The last two Browning-Chaney collaborations indicated that the horror cycle was on the wane. Audiences were confronted with the prospect of talking pictures and because of the interest in and growth of radio, were being subjected to a new kind of drama.

West of Zanzibar, adapted from the stage play *Kongo*, was directed by Browning and incorporated some of his dramatic touches, but it was essentially a filmization of the play. Chaney interpreted the character with his usual competence, enhancing it with realism by his ability to make seem easy that which was physically difficult. He seemed to be actually a man whose legs were paralyzed, and since this condition was part of the plot, and not contrived to show off his ability to portray deformity, his characterization was a more integrated one.

There was an element of strength in all of Chaney's performances. He dominated, whether by his appearance in make-up, the essence of physical strength he projected, or by strength of character. If some of his performances were not satisfactory it was because of weakness in the story or control exercised over the whole production.

Where East Is East was one of the least successful of the collaborative efforts of the star and director-writer. The formula was wearing thin. If the film had been made three years earlier it might have had more vitality and been better accepted by an audience which, whether they realized it or not, had been exposed to a new Chaney,

Lon Chaney and Lupe Velez.

Publicity still.

an actor whose ability and subtlety of characterization could be demonstrated without contrived situations or story twists.

The studio, in an effort to sustain the popular image of its star as a Man of a Thousand Faces, allowed him this vehicle to demonstrate his craftsmanship as a make-up artist. The scars he devised were exceptional in their realism.

No one could be sure what direction the industry would take, or what the public would expect, and demand. The talkies changed the public taste and the studios' projects. Chaney's roles during this period were varied enough to indicate that he would be able to adapt to whatever kind of film the studio might concentrate on.

There were several roles that he played that were more in the classical vein than either contemporary or popular. These were in prestige pictures (or art films). There was more emphasis on the total picture than on a vehicle for a star. The first of these, and the first picture of the newly-formed studio, was calculated to be impressive, to indicate the high quality of film that could be expected.

Gathered together were a top star (Chaney), a top director (Viktor Sjöström, americanized to Victor Seastrom) of the European school, and a play of emotional intensity. The results were impressive.

How the film *He Who Gets Slapped* and Chaney's performance were received when released can best be illustrated by quotes from the review in the *New York Times* of November 10, 1924:

> It is a shadow drama so beautifully told, so flawlessly directed that we might imagine that it will be held up as a model by all producers. Throughout its length there is not an instant of ennui, not a second one wants to lose . . . Never in his efforts before the camera has Mr. Chaney delivered such a marvelous performance as he does as this character. He is restrained in his acting, never overdoing the sentimental situation, and is guarded in his make-up.

Lon Chaney, Norma Shearer, and Claire McDowell.

The Tower of Lies was the second of Seastrom's efforts with Chaney as star and was perhaps not so successful for him because of the emphasis on pictorial story-telling. He had done between these two both *The Unholy Three* and *The Phantom of the Opera*, which more emphasized the characterizations with which he was identified. That he could accept any film assignment and do a competent job there is no doubt but there were some in which his talents and identification with the role were more inspired.

His make-up for this role as the Swedish peasant was criticized, but upon close examination it was as close to the real thing as could be imagined. The essence was there and in the fantasy world of the film, reality must sometimes be suggested rather than starkly portrayed. The story, the settings, and the emphasis on camera work limited Chaney somewhat in depicting a character with his usual strength. In both these films he was more restrained.

The selection of film roles was difficult. Care had to be taken that they emphasized the star's strong points. To let him portray characters that were formulized and had no substance might tire an audience whose appetite was voracious yet could easily become jaded. The artistic films were interspersed with those in which he played grotesque roles and straight dramatic roles.

Mr. Wu was an adaptation of a popular stage play that had been performed on Broadway in 1914 and prior to that in England. The film version had elaborate sets and costumes and was updated to present a picture of Chinese life and morality acceptable to American audiences of 1927. The story, which mainly concerns the young mandarin, was expanded to include other characters in order to give Chaney the opportunity of portraying not only one Oriental, but three of different ages.

Chaney was excellent as the mandarin whose daughter had been wronged by an Englishman. He was able to make believable the emotions of a man of the East, educated in the West, having to destroy his own daughter, wreak vengeance on her despoiler, and by a twist of fate, swallow poison that the mother of the young man intended for herself.

In *Laugh, Clown, Laugh,* which was also based on a stage play, Chaney played the unhappy clown. The whole atmosphere was one of fantasy. The middle-aged clown is gloomy; a young count cannot control his giggling. A doctor advises them to find a wholesome love, and they go on tour with the circus. The clown, in love with his young ward, is hurt and angry when he discovers the two young

Here is the young Mandarin Wu with Mrs. Gregory (Louise Dresser), mother of the young man who has trifled with Wu's daughter.

people are in love. The show must go on, and the clown does his famous "slide for life," balancing on his head on a wire stretched from the balcony to the stage. The wire is faulty and the clown falls to his death.

This was said to be Chaney's favorite role. There are similarities to Quasimodo: the mask that hides unrequited love, and sacrifice that the loved one may find happiness. Any weaknesses in the film, and in Chaney's performance, were due to the story rather than in its presentation.

Mockery was another film that might be considered prestige only because it was directed by the Danish Benjamin Christensen. Hollywood imported many European actors and directors in the hope of adding lustre to its productions. Written also by Christensen, it was

Lon Chaney and Nils Asther.

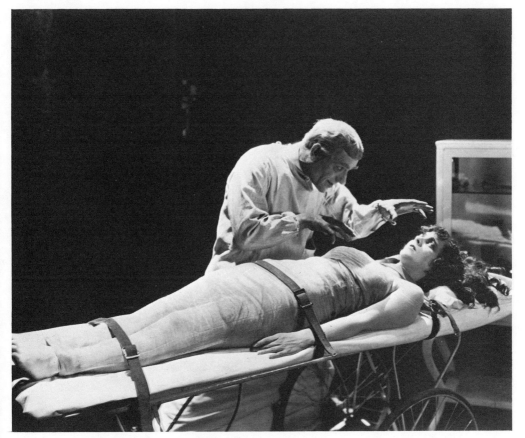

Dr. Ziska about to perpetrate some surgical villainy on Gertrude Olmsted.

no distinguished effort, being sometimes ponderous and illogical. The most interesting thing was Chaney's make-up as a Russian peasant, which was well conceived for the part. His performance was far better than the film deserved.

The remainder of Chaney's M-G-M films were changes-of-pace. *The Monster,* in spite of the implications of its title, was more slapstick than horror, and one could not be sure Chaney took the whole thing seriously. In *While the City Sleeps* he played, with no make-up, a detective; in *Thunder,* his last silent movie, he was an old man, a railroad engineer. In each he was thoroughly competent.

In one film, *Tell It to the Marines,* appeared Chaney the actor. There was no make-up, no deformity, no psychological quirk. He was himself, and some say this was his finest role. He looked the

Chaney as the old engineer.

part of the tough Marine sergeant, and he brought to it those qualities of pride, discipline, and strength that the portrayal demanded. Not to underestimate his ability as an actor, he seemed here to be expressing his own personal convictions.

The Unholy Three of 1930 was Lon Chaney's first talkie and last film. Since it is the only film by which the speaking Chaney can be judged it becomes one of his most important. And, in a way, it stands as a glowing tribute to an actor who applied himself with total dedication and painstaking care to his profession. Although tragic and ironic, it is perhaps fitting that the man dying of throat cancer should have ended his career with such a vocal triumph.

Many prefer the silent version for its tautness and increasing dramatic tension. If the talkie has less of this it is replaced by the anticipation of watching and hearing a new Chaney. The broad pantomime

Publicity portrait in dress uniform of the Marine Corps.

The sweet, old pet-shop owner in the sound version of **The Unholy Three.** Chaney's disguise as the old lady differed little from the earlier silent film.

of the silents had to be subordinated to adapt to the technique of
dialogue expressing emotion without having actors appear stiff and
static. Chaney seemed so much at ease that any of the rumors about
his being apprehensive about talkies must have been unfounded,
or misinterpreted.

His voice was a pleasant surprise. It was deep and virile, quite
appropriate to his personality, and it was flexible. That he examined
its use as thoroughly as he had examined make-up is apparent. His
years of experience on the stage had taught him something of voice
projection and he conferred with professional voice coaches. As his
movements had the grace of a dancer, so his voice adopted the
techniques of a singer.

Chaney signed affidavits stating that it was his voice that was
used for the several characters he portrayed in the film. Voice
dubbing would have had to be far more advanced for it to have

Publicity still from the sound version of **The Unholy Three.**

The Unholy Three of 1930: Ivan Linow, Harry Earles, and Lon Chaney.

been otherwise. In the opening scenes of the film the camera (and sound) follows the barker—or spieler, or announcer—around the carnival as he introduces the various sideshow acts. When he introduces Professor Echo, the ventriloquist, Chaney goes into a short routine with his ventriloquist's dummy, even throwing his voice into the audience. While he is talking, in his several voices, the camera picks up the movement of the muscles in his throat and the very slight movement of his lips.

The voice he uses as a performer is soft and smooth. When he talks to his fellows in crime it takes on a harsh, hard sound. When he is speaking as the sweet old lady pet shop owner, his voice is high pitched and slightly tremulous. This was a delicate part of Chaney's portrayal.

There were moments when what was intended to be humorous could have become ludicrous. Several times he had to do a quick change to the old lady. The action provided a temporary relief from tension for the audience, whose attention was immediately snapped back to the relationships of the characters to each other in each particular scene.

The courtroom scene near the end of the film makes it quite apparent that Chaney is using his own voice throughout. The old lady is in the witness box being questioned by the prosecuting attorney. As she gives her testimony she inadvertently drops her assumed voice to normal.

A review of *The Unholy Three* said:

> Mr. Chaney has made a further contribution to the modern

Ivan Linow, Lila Lee, and Lon Chaney.

The courtroom scene toward the end of **The Unholy Three.** Chaney's timid and apprehensive old lady disguise is penetrated when, during intense questioning by the prosecuting attorney (John Miljan), his assumed voice drops to his normal one. Chaney's considerable vocal achievement in this film assured his future in talkies. His untimely death denied motion pictures a new Lon Chaney, a "Man of a Thousand Voices."

motion picture—although it may be a bit indelicate to mention it here. Like the two dozen students who swam the Hellespont and so ruined the beautiful legend forever, he has destroyed the effect of the phrase, "See your favorite actor; he speaks." For while others were loudly proclaiming the finding of a forgotten note, he quietly went fishing and came back with five. The industry will never be the same again.

The Actor

To assess Lon Chaney as an actor necessarily requires a method of comparison. The question is how the comparison is to be made, and with whom. Chaney's work as compared to his contemporaries established him as unique. But this niche often obscured his real worth as an actor. It cannot be denied that he was an actor, even a great one. His fame and reputation rested on a few roles, yet his professionalism was evident in all he did. He approached each role with the thoroughness and competence that distinguishes the professional. There were imitators and acclaimed successors but none was successful as such. Those whose work was reminiscent of Chaney's most remembered efforts became personalities of their own and established their own following among the movie audiences of the particular period. Even Chaney's son, who changed his name to Lon Chaney, Jr., became a part of the cycle of films produced by studios to capitalize on the current vogue of horror. Although never a star he performed some admirable character parts in his almost forty-year acting career in over one hundred and fifty films.

The differences between actors are greater and easier to point out than certain subtle qualities that are not so readily apparent. If at first there seems to be no basis for comparison, further examination reveals certain qualities in common. There is little to suggest a comparison with, for example, Vincent Price, who found a place in the

Lon Chaney and his famous make-up box. The actor's make-up kit was the fore-runner of the make-up departments of the film studios. Chaney was a pioneer in the field. The materials that he used seem almost primitive compared to those that have been developed since his time, but the artistry and ingenuity of the man transcended the limitations of his materials.

milieu of psychological horror. The two are separated by appearance, background, personality, and by time, a generation of time, during which the tastes of the public changed and the medium changed.

Chaney was an average-sized man, not handsome, with an unpolished look. Price is tall, handsome, and distinguished looking. Chaney had not the benefit of a formal education and he traveled the hard road to success. Price was educated in America and Europe. Chaney was reticent, not given to public appearances. Price is gregarious and is at ease in any medium.

Both appreciated art, however it was manifested. Price's interest is in painting and the arts in general. He pursued acting as creative outlet when he felt he was not good enough at painting. Chaney directed his creativity to the artistry of make-up and characterization.

The film performances of each have a certain similarity, particularly in those roles that depict personalities not always predictable. The interpretations of the roles stressed different aspects of the characters, yet brought into focus motivational forces necessary to portray those characters. The series of Chaney films directed by Tod Browning and those of Vincent Price that were based on Edgar Allen Poe's tales have much in common. They were stories of the grotesque and imagination. The aspect of terror was present, and each actor interpreted his role with his own unique ability. Each of the actors maintained an artistic integrity in his approach to the roles. If at times there seemed to be a lessening of effort it was more that the vehicle could not support the weight of the actor, and not because the actor had let down his standards.

Chaney dedicated himself to all the fine attention to detail he considered the roles called for, and which he felt his audiences expected of him. The products of the studio also carried the stamp of quality, even though in a sense they were products of an assembly line, and were expected to make money. Chaney had to probably work harder at his roles than most actors simply because of the high standards he set for himself. Each step in his career had been the result of hard work and devotion to an ideal of craftsmanship. He perhaps felt he could not make a step forward without thoroughly examining the ground before him.

The nature of many of his roles was such that where the physical was emphasized, the psychological was less apparent but was nevertheless probed deeply. The audiences expected the visual shock, and if they came away impressed by other, more subtle feelings, it was because he knew his characters so well.

Vincent Price is an accomplished and professional actor who moves through his performances with such apparent ease and assurance that audiences are not always aware of the quality of his work. His interpretations of his roles in the terror category were based on the psychological, with gesture and expression indicating the disturbed mind, without relying on the twisted body for effect. Costuming and macabre sets added to the total effect.

It is sometimes difficult to differentiate between the creative artist and the craftsman. The artist must use imagination and try to avoid a formula so that his work has freshness and vitality. The craftsman must be thoroughly grounded in his craft so his techniques are flawless even if somewhat formulized. Chaney's acting combined the qualities of both artist and craftsman.

The Portrayals

I t is regrettable that portraits from Chaney's early films are so scarce. In many he played roles that required character make-up of some kind. It is unfortunate, too, that so many of his films lapsed into obscurity because of their very nature. Until he gained real prominence in *The Miracle Man*, his efforts were overshadowed by the super-stars such as Pickford, Fairbanks, and Chaplin.

Make-up in the early days of the films was almost non-existent. Whatever was used was a carry-over from the stage. Most filming was done out of doors, so there was little need for the kind of make-up now so necessary, except for the usual beards and moustaches to denote villains. The characters in the early films were pretty much the stereotyped ones created on the stage and did not have much subtlety until the films became more ambitious projects, telling stories and depending more on realism. When the producing companies built studios to shoot pictures in, the filming techniques were improved, finding new ways to use the camera and lighting.

It would hardly do for the leading players to be shown in close-up, magnified many times on the screen, with skin blemishes or unflattering highlights and shadows. It was obvious that make-up had to be used, but the materials for the stage would not do. Both Max Factor and George Westmore developed grease paints whose application and color qualities lent greater reality than the natural skin tones when photographed under the existing lighting and film conditions. As film techniques improved so did the make-up.

In the mid-twenties special make-up departments were set up in the studios. Prior to that time actors did their own make-up; those who were the most proficient did it for the others. All make-up is essentially character make-up, but the most interesting and most difficult is that which transforms an actor into someone else. The "someone else" can be due to the aging process, or metamorphosis, such as from man to monster, or the recreation of a character in a novel or an historical figure.

During the latter half of the 1920s a group of actors who had been doing make-up for everyone else got together and formed the Motion Picture Make-Up Artists Association and began to charge for their services. Also the Society of Motion Picture Engineers conducted a series of tests to standardize colors of make-up and the film and lighting. It was found that the make-up colors were no longer suitable for the newer type of film and lights, so Max Factor created a new range of colors called panchromatic make-up.

Lon Chaney was one of the pioneers in the field, and his efforts called attention to the importance and potentially lucrative business of cosmetics.

In order to classify Lon Chaney's screen portrayals the most obvious feature of each characterization is used as basis for the category. Some of his roles demanded more than one technique; for example in *The Road to Mandalay* he used a blind eye and scars. In other roles the characterization was such that the passing of time or some personal experience caused changes in the appearance of the character. In many of his films Chaney portrayed more than one character, consequently examples in several categories are from one film.

Since a picture was not shot in the same sequence as the plot evolved the scenes requiring a particular kind of make-up could be done at the same time. Obviously many scenes took several days to complete, so a great deal of care had to be taken that the make-up was exactly the same day after day. Lon Chaney's artistry becomes more apparent with the realization that he could not resort to plastic masks prepared in advance but had to apply a new make-up each time.

The portraits shown here illustrate Chaney's physical interpretations as well as his use of the various techniques of facial make-up,

Quasimodo, the Hunchback of Notre Dame.

Quasimodo and Esmeralda (Patsy Ruth Miller).

singly or in combination. Although the photographs are not in chronological order, it is still possible to note the development and refinement of his artistry. The first shown are his two classic portrayals, Quasimodo and Erik, the Phantom of the Opera.

THE HUNCHBACK OF NOTRE DAME

If Lon Chaney were to be remembered by only one screen portrayal, it would be as Quasimodo in *The Hunchback of Notre Dame*, for it embodied all the elements of characterization, facial and physical as well as psychological and emotional. The hunchback was created by wearing a harness-like appliance, with shoulder pads that held molded rubber humps in front and back to simulate the deformity, that held his body so he could not stand erect. A skin-like,

rubber covering over the seventy-pound device was tufted with hair on the shoulders, arms, and chest. The scene of Quasimodo on the whipping wheel shows the startling effect of the costume. It is said that for the scene Chaney told the actor who was to do the whipping not to hold back but make it look real.

The nose, eye, and cheekbones were built up with plasto, or mortician's wax, and the jagged false teeth fitted with wire to keep the mouth open. The whole face was covered with a heavy layer of grease paint. A dirty-looking, matted wig and bristly eyebrows completed the make-up.

Victor Hugo's description was faithfully recreated:

> . . . that tetrahedron nose, of that horseshoe mouth, of that little left eye, stubbled up with an eyebrow of carroty bristles while the right was completely overwhelmed and buried by an enor-

Quasimodo chained to the whipping wheel.

mous wen; of those irregular teeth, jagged here and there like the battlements of a fortress; of that horny lip, over which one of those teeth protruded, like the tusk of an elephant; of that forked chin; and above all of the expression, that mixture of spite, wonder, and melancholy . . . his prodigious head was covered with red bristles; between his shoulders rose an enormous hump, which was counterbalanced by a protuberance in front; his thighs and legs were so strangely put together that they touched at no one point but the knees, and seen in front, resembled two sickles joined at the handles; his feet were immense, his hands monstrous; but, with all this deformity there was a formidable air of strength, agility, and courage . . . he looked like a giant who had been broken to pieces and ill soldered together.

Hugo also stresses "Quasimodo's naked hump, his camel breast, and his scaly and hairy shoulders" when he is on the whipping wheel.

THE PHANTOM OF THE OPERA

This was one of Chaney's most startling costumes; a simulation of a death's head. Much of all make-up depends on the highlights and shadows created by the lighting conditions that accent the effect of the grease paint. Erik's high forehead, created by a built-up head-piece, sparse hair and taped-back ears elongated the whole face. The deep eye sockets were made by darkening the eye area; and to emphasize the eyeballs the upper portion of the lower lid was highlighted. The nose was uptilted, probably by a narrow strip of fishskin pulled up and attached to the bridge and the nostrils widened with wire inserts and outlined with dark paint. The cheekbones were built up with putty and the cheeks darkened to accentuate the gauntness of the face. The teeth molded of gutta percha, were jagged and the mouth was accented. A dark, tightly-fitting suit completed the skeletal appearance.

The creator of the character, Gaston Leroux, describes Erik in the novel:

He is extraordinarily thin and his dress coat hangs on a skeleton frame. His eyes are so deep that you can hardly see the fixed pupils. You just see two big black holes, as in a dead man's skull. His skin, which is stretched across his bones like a drumhead, is

Erik.

Erik, the Phantom of the Opera.

not white, but a nasty yellow. His nose is so little talking about that you can't see it sideface; and *the absence* of that nose is a horrible thing *to look at*. All the hair he has is three or four long dark locks on his forehead and behind his ears.

When the Phantom appeared at the masked ball at the Paris

Opera in his gruesome disguise as the Red Death:

It was a man all dressed in scarlet, with a huge hat and feathers

The Red Death.

Lon Chaney as the fake cripple, Frog, in **The Miracle Man.**

on the top of a wonderful death's head. From his shoulders hung an immense red-velvet cloak, which trailed along the floor like a king's train.

THE CRIPPLES

In his portrayal of Frog in *The Miracle Man,* Chaney's emphasis was on the physical. Here he was given his first important opportunity to play the kind of role he was to make uniquely his own. There was little facial make-up required, except for the unshaven and unkempt look. There is no doubt that the role showed Chaney the tremendous possibilities for this type of characterization. The scene where the fake cripple drags himself, painfully and slowly, up the path towards the Patriarch, to the point of the "miracle" where this body, so crippled, begins slowly and painfully, to unwind itself and stand erect held the audience tense with emotion, although it was a scene used again and again in other pictures.

The author of the novel *The Miracle Man*, Frank L. Packard, describes Frog, or the Flopper as he is there called, as

a misshapen thing, bulking a black blotch in the night at the entrance of the dark alleyway—like some lurking creature in its lair. He neither stood, nor kneeled, nor sat—no single word would describe his posture—he combined all three in a sort of repulsive, formless heap.

The Flopper moved. He came out from the alleyway onto the pavement, into the lurid lights of the Bowery, flopping along knee to toe on one leg, dragging the other behind him—and the leg he dragged was limp and wobbled from the knee. One hand sought the pavement to balance himself and aid in locomotion; the other arm, the right, was twisted out from his body in the shape of an inverted V, the palm of his hand, with half-curled, contorted fingers, almost touching his chin, as his head sagged at a stiff, set angle into his right shoulder. Hair straggled from the brim of a nondescript felt hat onto his eyes, and curled, dirty and unshaven, around his ears and the nape of his neck. His face was covered with a stubble of four days' growth, his body with rags— a coat; a shirt, the button long since gone at the neck; and trousers gaping in wide rents at the knees, and torn at the ankles where they flapped around miss-mated socks and shoes.

Chaney played cripples in other, later films. One of the most noteworthy was the Bishop in *The Blackbird* and, of course, the famous legless man in *The Penalty*.

THE BLACKBIRD

The paralytic posture assumed by Chaney for this film was one of his most difficult. It took an incredible effort to keep one side of his body motionless while contorting his other limbs. All of this required intense concentration, for any small movement would have destroyed the illusion. The visual effect of the role was so fascinating that one never thought to wonder how the character could get his clothes on or off.

The Bishop unbent.

THE UNKNOWN

Chaney created his armless man by wearing a leather corset that bound his arms tightly to his body. A further deformity of the man was a double thumb.

WEST OF ZANZIBAR

To portray the paraplegic who moved about in a wheel chair or dragged himself about on the floor, Chaney needed touches of realism. In addition to his shaved head and soiled clothes, even his fingernails were dirty.

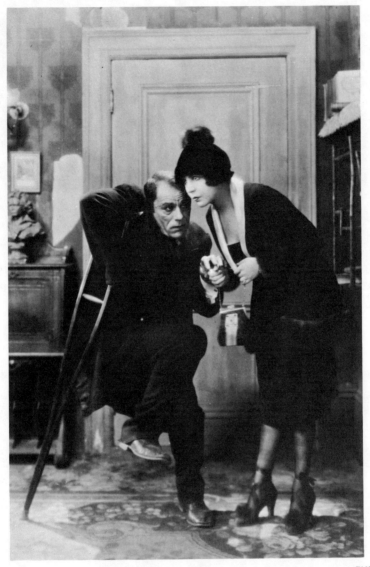

Lon Chaney as the crippled Bishop in **The Blackbird**. Renee Adoree as Fifi.

THE PENALTY

Chaney was often accused of being double-jointed but he was not. His body was flexible and he was strong, yet in later years he did suffer some back trouble no doubt brought on by binding his limbs for roles such as this.

This scene from **The Unknown** shows how Chaney's arms were bound tightly to his body. Cojo (John George) does the lacing.

Lon Chaney and Mary Nolan.

Lon Chaney as the paraplegic in **West of Zanzibar.** The shaved head, dirty clothes, and even dirty finger nails are appropriate to the character.

Portrait of Blizzard in **The Penalty.**

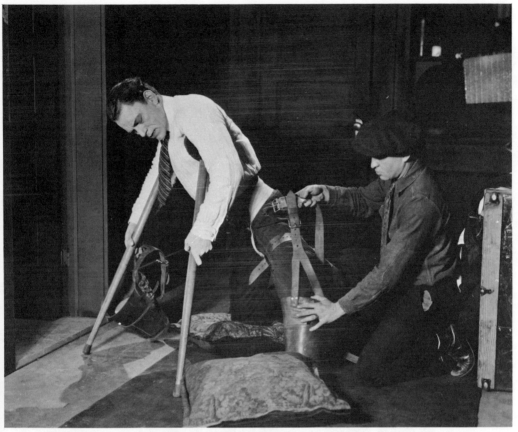

Lon Chaney preparing for his role of the legless man in **The Penalty.** If the film audiences never quite believed what they saw, Chaney never spared himself to achieve the proper effect.

BLIND

The blind pirate Pew of the film *Treasure Island* was not the short-lived pirate of Stevenson's novel, although he was modelled closely after him. Despite some difference in dress, the screen portrait was the essence of the character. The costuming created the image, but the false teeth, bushy eyebrows and straggly hair intensified the characterization.

Stevenson describes Pew as seen by the young boy Jim Hawkins:

I saw someone drawing slowly near along the road. He was

Lon Chaney as the blind pirate Pew in **Treasure Island**.

plainly blind, for he tapped before him a stick, and wore a great green shade over his eyes and nose; and he was hunched, as if with age or weakness, and wore a huge old tattered sea-cloak with a hood, that made him appear positively deformed. I never saw in my life a more dreadful looking figure . . . I never heard a voice so cruel, and cold, and ugly as that blind man's. . . . He suddenly left hold of me, and, with incredible accuracy and nimbleness, skipped out of the parlour and into the road.

To depict blindness was a more difficult matter. Today all that would be needed would be appropriate contact lenses, but no such thing was available in the early actor's make-up box. The effect could be achieved by rolling back the eyes, but only for a short time. One of the methods attributed to Chaney in *The Road to Mandalay* was the use of collodion, a viscous liquid consisting of a solution of alcohol and ether in which soluble guncotton or pyroxylin is dissolved and forms an adhesive film. But collodion could be dangerous. It seems more likely that he used the thin, opaque, white skin from inside the shell of an egg to cover his eye. It is uncomfortable but not painful. Cecil Holland describes the method in his book on make-up.

SCARRED AND DISFIGURED

Scars and other facial blemishes, such as pock marks, were usually created by applications of collodion in proper density. Collodion is irritating to the skin but gives a remarkably realistic effect. Cuts, raised scars, bruises, and burns were made with plasto wax. Chaney used scars in many of his roles, notably the chest scars in *Mockery*, those around the blind eye in *The Road to Mandalay*, and the tiger claw marks in *Where East Is East*.

Chaney's make-up for Ricardo in *Victory* included not only pock marks and a scar over his right eye, but heavily accented brows and a black, drooping moustache.

Joseph Conrad describes the character in his novel as "a muscular, short man with eyes that gleamed and blinked, a harsh voice, and a round, tone-less, pock-marked face ornamented by a thin, disheveled moustache sticking out quaintly under the tip of a rigid nose."

Lon Chaney as Sergei in **Mockery**.

Singapore Joe, one of Chaney's most startling make-up effects. The blind eye is further accentuated by the scars around it and by the painted blood vessels. Each of his roles was a challenge to his ingenuity, to go beyond what would have been merely acceptable. He made constant demands on himself, refusing to let his art deteriorate. But he never used a make-up for its effect alone, it was only a part of the characterization.

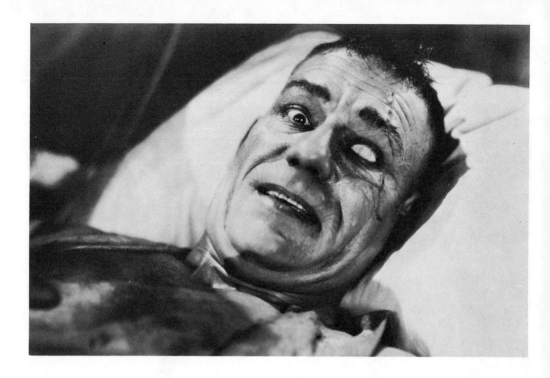

Chaney's collodion scars were remarkably realistic. Estelle Taylor's Oriental make-up illustrates the eye treatment generally used to depict the Oriental type.

Lon Chaney as Tiger Haynes in **Where East Is East.**

Lon Chaney and Seena Owen in **Victory.** The pock-marks and the scar were made with collodion. Realism was very important to Chaney. As his career progressed he drew his characterizations from real life rather than relying on the accepted stereotypes.

ORIENTAL

Some of the most interesting characters to come out of Chaney's make-up box were his Chinese. To slant the eyes narrow strips of fishskin were affixed with spirit gum to the outer edges of the lids. A narrow strip of adhesive tape or thread was attached first to one piece of fishskin, drawn over the back of the head with enough tension to slant the eye, and then attached to the other side. The upper lids and brows were covered either with putty or with a thin layer of cotton. If the nose required broadening, it was done by inserting cut-off ends of cigar holders into the nostrils. The mouth was pursed by using irregular and slightly protruding false teeth made

Grandfather Wu.

Here Chaney represents the middle-aged Wu, the son and father. The signs of age are beginning to show.

Wu and his daughter Nang Ping (Renee Adoree).

of gutta percha and painted with enamel to create the desired effect. Chaney's ancient grandfather in *Mr. Wu* is one of his most interesting creations. Here, in addition to the painted wrinkles and wispy beard, the effect of wizened age is further heightened by the oversized spectacles and the enormous folds of the dark hood, utilizing lights and shadows.

The novel by Louise Jordan Miln, based on the stage play *Mr. Wu*, gives scant description of the character. The old mandarin is described in such scattered phrases as "eighty" and "gaunt, withered, pockmarked."

Besides three different faces in *Mr. Wu*, Chaney created various Chinese make-ups for *Outside the Law, Bits of Life,* and *Shadows.*

Chaney's Oriental in **Outside the Law** is an example of the thoroughness with which he approached his characterizations. He paid great attention to details—teeth, mouth, eyes, hair, and even expression and posture.

Bits of Life was a 1921 Marshall Neilan film comprising four separate stories, the third of which, "Hop," starred Chaney and Anna May Wong. Here was a further development of his Oriental characterization.

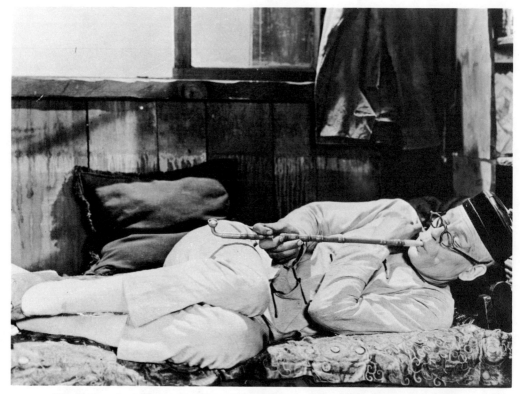

The Chinese laundryman of Wilbur Daniel Steele's short story was one of Chaney's finest characterizations. **Shadows** was selected as one of the best pictures of 1922 by Robert E. Sherwood, along with such films as Fairbanks' **Robin Hood** and Valentino's **Blood and Sand.** Chaney's acting, in addition to his fine make-up, made him seem physically smaller and frail while projecting great inner strength. He used his marvelously expressive hands to great effect.

CLOWNS

In *He Who Gets Slapped* Chaney played a scientist, adorned with aristocratic beard and moustache, who escapes into the world of make-believe by hiding his newly-shaven face and his worldly disappointments behind the comic-tragic mask of the clown. The clown make-up, itself a classic conception, has an individuality and ingeniousness that apparently tempted Chaney. For this role and that in *Laugh, Clown, Laugh,* he studied and examined carefully the traditional white-face.

Studies of Chaney's clown make-up for **He Who Gets Slapped.**

Director Herbert Brenon and Lon Chaney in a publicity photo for **Laugh, Clown, Laugh.**

Loretta Young, Cissy Fitzgerald, Lon Chaney, and Bernard Seigel in **Laugh, Clown, Laugh.** It was said this was Chaney's favorite film. The clown character is a traditional and universal one, and offers the actor great latitude combining, as it does, such a full emotional range. It offered Chaney the opportunity of creating a unique clown make-up, as well as extending his pantomimic skill beyond the limits of the silent screen. The classic concept of the broken heart behind the smiling face let him take his place with the most famous **Pagliacci.**

GROTESQUE AND SINISTER

Many of Chaney's roles had aspects of the grotesque and sinister, although some were closer to beasts than men. In *The Blind Bargain* the creature produced by glandular surgery is more ape than human. The close-cropped hair, pointed head, low forehead, broad nose and thick lips, were set upon the crouched body of an animal.

One of the most grotesque of Chaney's roles was the Ape Man in the 1922 **The Blind Bargain.** In this film he played two roles: the scientist Dr. Lamb, who experimented with glandular transplants, and the pathetic ape man, the result of one of those experiments. In this make-up, as in the later **Mockery,** Chaney created bestiality by thickening the lips, broadening the nose, and extending the brows across the bridge of the nose. In this instance the hair, brought low over the forehead, was coarse and close cropped. He moved his hunched, half-man body with simian agility.

The sinister Dr. Ziska in **The Monster.** In this 1925 film Chaney used a relatively simple make-up but his characterization also made use of grimace, gesture, and eerie atmosphere; although the make-up is largely limited to the use of a hair-piece, the total character approaches the grotesque.

Study of the peasant in **Mockery**.

The sinister surgeon in *The Monster* has an inhuman quality, though his make-up is milder. For him the emphasis is on situation and posturing. Chaney's creation suits the asylum-like atmosphere where comedy and terror are combined.

In *Mockery* Chaney used make-up to create a character of limited mental ability. He relied on a low forehead and heavy brows joined together over the broad nose to achieve the effect. The long hair and stubble beard, the scars on the chest, the peasant costume, and the posture completed the illusion of a man whose body was stronger than his mind.

The murder mystery *London After Midnight* gave Chaney a dual role. The Scotland Yard inspector was a scholarly-looking and capable detective, who led the murderer to his downfall. The vampire, one of Chaney's most frightening characters, is one of the instruments used to solve the crime. The sharply-pointed false teeth had small wires attached to raise the corners of the mouth into a fixed grin. The top hat covering the long wispy hair, and the cape that resembled a bat's wings when spread out accented the sinister. In addition to the dark make-up around the eyes and the rounded brows, to create the hypnotic stare it has been said that Chaney used chemicals to dilate his pupils, making it extremely difficult to work under the bright studio lights. It also has been said he tightened fine wires across his eyelids to make his eyes protrude.

Scotland Yard Inspector Burke (Chaney) and the murderer Sir James Hamlin (H. B. Walthall).

The vampire.

Marcelline Day and Lon Chaney examine the contents of the vampire's make-up box.

AGE

The ways of making a man look old are many and varied. The make-up must indicate the age as well as the physical characteristics. Grey or white hair was indicated by dusting starch or aluminum powder on the natural hair or by using false hair. The thick and bristly eyebrows of the aged were made with crepe hair or by whitening the natural brows with mascara. Wrinkles were created by accenting the skin lines or by drawing additional lines with a lining pencil. For the very old, wrinkled skin was created by applying a heavy coating of a mixture of grease paint and putty into which criss-cross lines were engraved with a fine-pointed stylus.

The characters in a film age differently, depending on their situ-

A study depicting age.

Lon Chaney as the railroad engineer in **Thunder**.

Fagin (Lon Chaney) teaches young Oliver (Jackie Coogan) the art of picking pockets in the 1922 **Oliver Twist**. The Artful Dodger (Edouard Trebaol) and Charley Bates (Taylor Graves) look on. Chaney's make-up was a frightening one, especially to the nine-year-old Coogan. It was reported that when Chaney came onto the set Jackie ran away screaming.

ation. The actor must determine how he can reveal the personality and background of the character. Chaney's portrayal of Fagin in *Oliver Twist* emphasized the universality rather than the specific nationality depicted by Dickens or George Cruikshank, one of his illustrators. Dickens described Fagin as having a "very old shrivelled . . . villainous-looking and repulsive face . . . obscured by a quantity of matted red hair."

The character in *The Unholy Three* disguised as an old woman, with the white hair, wrinkles, a slight stoop, and the general de-

Victor McLaglan, Harry Earles, and Lon Chaney in his disguise as the sweet old lady in the 1925 version of **The Unholy Three**. Although this make-up was a disguise, intended only to fool the characters within the film and not the audience, Chaney nevertheless created a character that could have been believable to the audience.

The sweet old lady (Chaney) and the baby (Harry Earles).

Lon Chaney and Claire McDowell in **The Tower of Lies.**

The Emperor of Portugallia.

The old man in his emperor's garb.

meanor and expression of a kindly old lady, has a terrifying aspect. For the gentle mien is the shield behind which a criminal mind hides. This was a triple role for Chaney: the sideshow ventriloquist performing; the criminal planning his crimes; and the little old lady running a pet shop as front for criminal activity. The sound version broadened Chaney's acting range by allowing him to project the voices of the ventriloquist's dummy, the old lady, a parrot, and his own.

The interesting characterization of the old peasant in *The Tower of Lies* is realized not only by the white hair and beard and the wrinkles around the eyes and back of the neck, but by the dress and posture of a hard-working man of the soil. The very costume of the Emperor indicates the poor man's fantasy.

In the novel *The Emperor of Portugallia,* from which *The Tower of Lies* was adapted, Selma Lagerlof pictures the Emperor at church:

Henry B. Walthall and Lon Chaney in an early scene from **The Road to Mandalay.** At this point in the film Chaney plays a straight role, as opposed to his later blinded and scarred character. There is a touch of make-up, however, which indicates characterization. The dark, wavy hair tends to give the face a softer and more youthful look.

But now there sat at the head of this bench just such a great personage, his hands resting on a long silver-mounted stick, his head crowned with a high, green leather cap, while on his waistcoat glittered two large stars, one like gold, the other like silver.

HAIR—WIGS AND BEARDS

The most frequently used material for beards and moustaches was crepe (wool-crepe) hair. It came in braids of various colors and shades. Great care had to be taken for the growth to look nat-

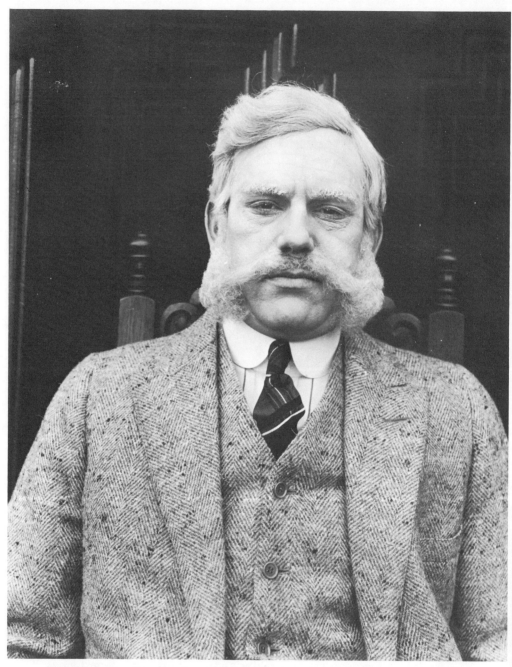

A study showing the use of crepe hair. Note the difference of texture of the hair and the Emperor Franz Joseph moustache.

In the days of vaudeville and in the early films, ethnic types were considered to possess certain characteristics that were exaggerated to the point of burlesque. This study shows the leprechaun qualities of the Irish make-up; bushy reddish hair and sideburns, heavy brows, laugh-lines at the eyes, long upper lip, and the quizzical expression.

Character study showing use of crepe hair.

ural and the color to be right so that it was indistinguishable from the natural hair when photographed. Spirit gum was used as an adhesive.

As Juan Serafin in **The Next Corner.** Reviewers said Chaney was wasted in a relatively minor role in this melodrama of marital difficulties set in contemporary (1924) Spain. This film was his last as a free-lance actor and perhaps best serves to illustrate that he could play straight dramatic roles as well as character parts. But after his tremendous success as **The Hunchback of Notre Dame,** he seemed out of place in modern dress and Valentino-like hair style.

Chaney used false hair with great skill, for both character parts and straight roles, especially in altering his hairline. Because of the nature of many of his roles he kept his own hair close-cropped.

STRAIGHT

The roles in which Lon Chaney appeared without make-up are as interesting as those in which he appeared with it. He was always

Chaney as the gangster Black Mike Silva in **Outside the Law.**

in character; his own personality was always subordinated. His mannerisms, gestures, expressions, belonged to the character, as did the small details of dress. The detective in *While the City Sleeps,*

Doris Lloyd and Lon Chaney in **The Blackbird.**

Chaney's gruff, tough Marine sergeant in **Tell It to the Marines** was one of his finest portrayals. As an actor he did not have to hide behind make-up to be effective.

Lon Chaney as the detective in **While the City Sleeps.**

The flashy-dressed gangster of **The Big City**. Nine years earlier Chaney and Betty Compson appeared together in **The Miracle Man**.

though neatly dressed, was probably too absorbed in his job to notice the spot on his vest, the result of a hurried breakfast. The crook in *The Big City*, on the other hand, seemed more concerned with his fancy clothes. Chaney used small details such as these to to give his characters life.

The Films

The check list of films begins with the first film in which Chaney received screen credit. Those made during the period 1913 to 1918 were made at Universal Studio under the names of the various production units there. The release dates do not always indicate the order in which they were made. For these early films the title, company, number of reels (2), release date (where sources are at variance the earliest date is used), and director where such information is available, are given.

Poor Jake's Demise
Imp (1) 8-16-13
Allen Curtis

The Sea Urchin
Powers (1) 8-22-13
Edwin August

The Trap
Powers (1) 10-3-13
Edwin August

Almost an Actress
Joker (1) 11-15-13
Allen Curtis

Back to Life
Victor (2) 11-24-13
Allan Dwan

Red Margaret, Moonshiner
Gold Seal (2) 12-9-13
Allan Dwan

Bloodhounds of the North
Gold Seal (2) 12-23-13
Allan Dwan

The Lie
Gold Seal (2) 1-6-14
Allan Dwan

The Honor of the Mounted
Gold Seal (2) 2-17-14
Allan Dwan

Remember Mary Magdelen
Victor (2) 2-23-14
Allan Dwan

Discord and Harmony
Gold Seal (3) 3-17-14
Allan Dwan

The Menace to Carlotta
Gold Seal (2) 3-22-14
Allan Dwan

The Embezzler
Gold Seal (2) 3-31-14
Allan Dwan

The Lamb, the Woman, the Wolf
101 Bison (3) 4-4-14
Allan Dwan

The End of the Feud
Rex (2) 4-12-14
Allan Dwan

*The Tragedy of
Whispering Creek*
101 Bison (2) 5-2-14
Allan Dwan

The Unlawful Trade
Rex (2) 5-14-14
Allan Dwan

The Forbidden Room
101 Bison (3) 6-20-14
Allan Dwan

The Old Cobbler
101 Bison (2) 6-27-14

Murdock MacQuarrie

A Ranch Romance
Nestor (2) 7-8-14

Her Grave Mistake
Nestor (2) 7-15-14

By the Sun's Rays
Nestor (2) 7-22-14

The Oubliette
101 Bison (3) 8-15-14
Charles Giblyn
(Note: First of four 3-reelers
comprising "The Adventures of
Francois Villon." Chaney also
appeared in the second, *The
Higher Law.*)

A Miner's Romance
Nestor (2) 8-26-14

Her Bounty
Rex (1) 9-13-14
Allan Dwan

Richelieu
101 Bison (4) 9-26-14
Allan Dwan

The Pipes of Pan
Rex (2) 10-4-14
Joseph DeGrasse

Virtue Is Its Own Reward
Rex (2) 10-11-14
Joseph DeGrasse

Her Life's Story
Rex (2) 10-15-14
Joseph DeGrasse

Lights and Shadows
Rex (2) 11-29-14
Joseph DeGrasse

The Lion, the Lamb, the Man
Rex (2) 12-6-14
Joseph DeGrasse

A Night of Thrills
Rex (2) 12-13-14
Joseph DeGrasse

Her Escape
Rex (2) 12-27-14
Joseph DeGrasse

The Sin of Olga Brandt
Rex (2) 1-3-15
Joseph DeGrasse

Star of the Sea
Rex (2) 1-10-15
Joseph DeGrasse

Threads of Fate
Rex (2) 1-14-15
Joseph DeGrasse

The Measure of a Man
Rex (2) 1-28-15
Joseph DeGrasse

*When the Gods Played
a Badger Game*
Rex (2) 2-28-15
Joseph DeGrasse

Such Is Life
Rex (2) 3-4-15
Joseph DeGrasse

Where the Forest Ends
Rex (2) 3-7-15
Joseph DeGrasse

All for Peggy
Rex (1) 3-8-15
Joseph DeGrasse

The Desert Breed
Rex (2) 3-13-15
Joseph DeGrasse

Outside the Gates
Rex (2) 3-14-15
Joseph DeGrasse

The Grind
Rex (3) 3-15-15
Joseph DeGrasse

Maid of the Mist
Rex (1) 3-19-15
Joseph DeGrasse

The Girl of the Night
Rex (2) 4-8-15
Joseph DeGrasse

The Stool Pigeon
Victor (2) 4-19-15
Lon Chaney

An Idyll of the Hills
Rex (2) 5-3-15
Joseph DeGrasse

For Cash
Victor (2) 5-3-15
Lon Chaney

The Stronger Mind
United (2) 5-15-15
Joseph DeGrasse

The Oyster Dredger
Victor (2) 6-14-15
Lon Chaney (also scenario)

Steady Company
Rex (1) 6-29-15
Joseph DeGrasse

The Violin Maker
Victor (1) 7-1-15
Lon Chaney

The Trust
Victor (1) 7-16-15
Lon Chaney

Bound on the Wheel
Rex (3) 7-19-15
Joseph DeGrasse

Mountain Justice
Rex (2) 8-15-15
Joseph DeGrasse

Quits
Rex (1) 8-17-15
Joseph DeGrasse

The Chimney's Secret
Victor (1) 8-25-15
Lon Chaney

The Pine's Revenge
Rex (2) 9-19-15
Joseph DeGrasse

*The Fascination of
the Fleur de Lis*
Rex (3) 9-26-15
Joseph DeGrasse

Alas and Alack
Rex (1) 10-10-15
Joseph DeGrasse

A Mother's Atonement
Rex (3) 10-17-15
Joseph DeGrasse

Lon of the Lone Mountain
Rex (1) 10-19-15
Joseph DeGrasse

The Millionaire Paupers
Rex (3) 10-26-15
Joseph DeGrasse

Father and the Boys
Broadway (5) 12-2-15
Joseph DeGrasse

Under a Shadow
Rex (2) 12-5-15
Joseph DeGrasse

Stronger Than Death
Rex (2) 12-17-15
Joseph DeGrasse

The Grip of Jealousy
Bluebird (5) 1-31-16
Joseph DeGrasse

Dolly's Scoop
Rex (2) 2-11-16
Joseph DeGrasse

Tangled Hearts
Bluebird (5) 3-8-16
Ida May Park

The Gilded Spider
Bluebird (5) 4-15-16
Joseph DeGrasse

Bobbie of the Ballet
Bluebird (5) 5-22-16
Joseph DeGrasse

Grasp of Greed
Bluebird (5) 6-17-16
Joseph DeGrasse

The Mark of Cain
Red Feather (5) 7-15-16
Joseph DeGrasse

*If My Country
Should Call*
Red Feather (5) 8-13-16
Joseph DeGrasse

Place Beyond the Winds
Red Feather (5) 10-25-16
Joseph DeGrasse

Felix on the Job
Victor (1) 10-31-16
George Felix

The Price of Silence
Bluebird (5) 12-1-16
Joseph DeGrasse

The Piper's Price
Bluebird (5) 12-26-16
Joseph DeGrasse

Hell Morgan's Girl
Bluebird (5) 3-5-17
Joseph DeGrasse

The Mask of Love
Big U (1) 3-29-17
Joseph DeGrasse

*The Girl in the
Checkered Coat*
Bluebird (5) 4-23-17
Joseph DeGrasse

The Flashlight Girl
Bluebird (5) 5-21-17
Ida May Park

A Doll's House
Bluebird (5) 6-7-17
Joseph DeGrasse

Fires of Rebellion
Bluebird (5) 7-2-17
Ida May Park

Vengeance of the West
Bluebird (5) 7-11-17
Joseph DeGrasse

The Rescue
Bluebird (5) 7-23-17
Ida May Park

Triumph
Bluebird (5) 8-14-17
Joseph DeGrasse

Pay Me
Jewel (5) 8-17-17
Joseph DeGrasse

The Empty Gun
Gold Seal (3) 9-4-17
Joseph DeGrasse

Anything Once
Bluebird (5) 10-8-17
Joseph DeGrasse

Bondage
Bluebird (5) 10-15-17
Ida May Park

The Scarlet Car
Bluebird (5) 12-24-17
Joseph DeGrasse

The last film made by Chaney while still a member of the Universal company was *That Devil Bateese*. Here again the release dates do not always indicate the order in which the films were made. His first film as a free-lance actor was *Riddle Gawne*.

The Grand Passion
Jewel (7) 1-12-18
Directed by Ida May Park
Scenario by Ida May Park from *The Boss of Powderville* by Thomas Addison.
Photographer King Grey.
Cast:

Dick Evans	William Stowell
Jack Ripley	Jack Mulhall
Viola	Dorothy Phillips
Red Pete	Bert Appling
Argos (Viola's father)	Lon Chaney
Boston Kate	Evelyn Selbie
Mackay	Alfred Allen

Broadway Love
Bluebird (5) 2-2-18
Directed by Ida May Park
Scenario by Ida May Park from a story by W. Carey Wonderley.
Cast:

Midge O'Hara	Dorothy Phillips
Cherry Blow	Juanita Hansen
Jack Chalvey	Harry Van Meter
Henry Rockwell	William Stowell
Elmer Watkins	Lon Chaney
Mrs. Watkins	Gladys Tennyson

The Kaiser, The Beast of Berlin
Renown (7) 3-14-18
Directed by Rupert Julian
Scenario by Rupert Julian and E. J. Clawson.
Cast:

The Kaiser	Rupert Julian
Capt. Von Neigle	Nigel de Brulier
Admiral Von Tirpitz	Lon Chaney
Capt. Von Hancke	Harry Van Meter
Ambassador Gerard	Joseph Girard
General Pershing	Henry Barrows
General Joffre	Harry Holden
Marcas, the Blacksmith	Elmo Lincoln
Belgian Women	⎧ Ruth Clifford ⎪ Billy Carpenter ⎨ Ruby Lafayette ⎪ Gretchen Lederer ⎩ Zoe Rae

Fast Company
Bluebird (5) 4-6-18
Directed by Lynn F. Reynolds
Scenario by Eugene Lewis and Waldemar Young from a story by John McDermott.
Cast:

Laurence Percival Van Huyler	Franklyn Farnum
Dan McCarty	Lon Chaney
Alicia Vanderveldt	Juanita Hansen
Mrs. Van Huyler	Katherine Griffith
Peter Van Huyler	Fred Montague
Richard Barnaby	Edward Cecil

A Broadway Scandal
Bluebird (5) 5-25-18
Directed by Joseph DeGrasse
Story by Harvey Gates.
Cast:

Nonette Bisson	Carmel Myers
Doctor Kendell	Edwin August
"Kink" Colby	Lon Chaney
Armand Bisson	Andrew Robson

That Devil Bateese
Bluebird (5) 9-2-18
Directed by William Wobert
Scenario by Bernard McConville from a story by Bess Meredith.
Cast:

Bateese Latour	Monroe Salisbury
Kathleen St. John	Ada Gleason
Martin Stuart	Lamar Johnstone
Louis Courteau	Lon Chaney
Father Pierre	Andrew Robson

The Talk of the Town
Bluebird (6) 9-23-18
Directed by Allan Holubar
From *Discipline of Ginevra* by Harold Vickers.
Cast:

Ginevra French	Dorothy Phillips
Laurence Tabor	William Stowell
Jack Lanchome	Lon Chaney
Major French	George Fawcett
Aunt Harriet	Clarissa Selwyn

Riddle Gawne
Paramount-Artcraft (5) 8-18-18
Directed by Lambert Hillyer
Scenario by William S. Hart from novel *The Vengeance of Jefferson Gawne* by Charles Alden Seltzer.
Photographer Joe August
Cast:

Riddle Gawne	William S. Hart
Kathleen Harkness	Katherine MacDonald
Hame Bozzam	Lon Chaney
Blanche Dillon	Gretchen Lederer
Jane	Gertrude Short
Jess Cass	Leon Kent
Reb Butler	Milton Ross
Colonel Harkness	Edwin B. Tilton

Danger—Go Slow
Universal Special (6) 12-9-18
Directed by Robert Z. Leonard

Story by Robert Leonard and Mae Murray.
Cast:

Muggsy Mulane	Mae Murray
Jimmy	Jack Mulhall
"Bud"	Lon Chaney
Judge Cotton	Joseph Girard
Jimmy's Mother	Lydia Knott

The Wicked Darling
Universal (6) 2-2-19
Directed by Tod Browning
Scenario by Harvey Gates from story by Evelyn Campbell.
Cast:

Mary Stevens (The Gutter Rose)	Priscilla Dean
Fadem	Spottiswood Aitken
Stoop Connors	Lon Chaney
Adele Hoyt	Gertrude Aster
Kent Mortimer	Wellington Playter

The False Faces
Paramount-Artcraft (7) 2-16-19
Directed by Irvin V. Willet
From the novel by Louis Joseph Vance.
Cast:

The Lone Wolf	Henry B. Walthall
Cecelia Brooks	Mary Anderson
Karl Eckstrom	Lon Chaney
Ralph Crane	Milton Ross
Lt. Thackeray	Thornton Edwards
Submarine Captain	William Bowman
Submarine Lieutenant	Carry McGarry
Blensop	Ernest Pasque

A Man's Country
Winsome—Robertson-Cole (5) 7-6-19
Directed by Henry Kolker
Story and scenario by John Lynch.
Cast:

Kate Carewe	Alma Rubens
Ralph Bowen	Albert Roscoe

"Three Card" Duncan	Lon Chaney
Marshall Leland	Joseph Dowling
Ruth Kemp	Edna May Wilson
Oliver Kemp	Alfred Hollingsworth
Connell	Phail Gastrock

Paid In Advance
Universal-Jewel (6) 7-6-19
Directed by Allen Holubar
Scenario by Allen Holubar, suggested by a story by James Oliver Curwood *The Girl Who Dared.*
Cast:

Joan	Dorothy Phillips
John Gray	Joseph Girard
Bateese Le Blanc	Lon Chaney
Marie	Priscilla Dean
Jim Blood	William Stowell
Gold Dust Barker	Frank Brownlee
Regan	Bill Burress
Flap Jack	Harry DeMore

The Miracle Man
Paramount-Artcraft (8) 8-31-19
Directed by George Loane Tucker
Scenario by George Loane Tucker from a novel by Frank L. Packard and play by George M. Cohan.
Cast:

Tom Burke	Thomas Meighan
Rose	Betty Compson
The Frog	Lon Chaney
The Dope	J. M. Dumont
Richard King	W. Lawson Butt
Claire King	Elinor Fair
Mr. Higgins	F. A. Turner
Ruth Higgins	Lucille Hutton
The Patriarch	Joseph Dowling

When Bearcat Went Dry
C. R. Macauley Photoplays (6) 10-25-19
Directed by Oliver Sellers

From the novel by Charles Neville Buck.
Cast:

Blossom Fulkerson	Vangie Valentine
Joel Fulkerson	Walt Whitman
Turner Stacey (Bearcat)	Bernard Durning
Lone Stacey	Winter Hall
Rattler Webb	Ed Brady
Jerry Henderson	M. K. Wilson
Kindard Powers	Lon Chaney

Victory
Paramount-Artcraft (8) 11-30-19
Directed by Maurice Tourneur
Scenario by Stephen Fox from novel by Joseph Conrad.
Photographer Rene Guissart.
Cast:

Axel Heyst	Jack Holt
Alma	Seena Owen
Ricardo	Lon Chaney
Shomberg	Wallace Beery
Mr. Jones	Ben Deely
Mrs. Shomberg	Laura Winston
Pedro	Bull Montana
Captain Davidson	George Nichols

Daredevil Jack
Pathe 2-15-20
Serial 15 episodes
Directed by W. S. Van Dyke
Scenario by Jack Cunningham from story by Frederic Chapin and
Harry Hoyt.
Cast:

Jack Dempsey
Josie Sedgewick
Lon Chaney
Spike Robinson
Ruth Langston
Hershall Mayall
Fred Starr
Frank Lamming
Albert Cody
Al Kaufman

Treasure Island
Paramount-Artcraft (6) 3-26-20
Directed by Maurice Tourneur
Scenario by Stephen Fox from novel by Robert Louis Stevenson.
Photographer Rene Guissart
Cast:

Jim Hawkins	Shirley Mason
Mrs. Hawkins	Josie Melville
Bill Bones	Al Filson
Black Dog	Wilton Taylor
Pew	Lon Chaney
Long John Silver	Charles Ogle
Israel Hands	Joseph Singleton
Morgan	Bull Montana
Merry	Lon Chaney
Captain Smollett	Harry Holden
Squire Trelawney	Sydney Dean
Dr. Livesey	Charles Hill Mailes

The Gift Supreme
C. R. Macauley Photoplays (6) 5-9-20
Directed by Oliver Sellers
From novel by George Allen England.
Cast:

Bradford Chandler Vinton	Bernard Durning
Eliot Vinton	Melbourne McDowell
Martha Vinton	Eugenie Besserer
Sylvia Alden	Seena Owen
Irving Stagg	Tully Marshall
Merney Stagg	Lon Chaney
Rev. Ebenezer Crowley Boggs	Jack Curtis
Dopey Dan	Dick Morris
Mrs. Wesson	Anna Dodge
Lalia Graun	Claire McDowell

Nomads of the North
Associated First National (6) 10-11-20
Directed by David M. Hartford
Scenario by David Hartford and James Oliver Curwood from novel
by James Oliver Curwood.

Photographer Walter Griffin
Cast:

Nanette Roland	Betty Blythe
Raoul Challoner	Lon Chaney
Corporal O'Conner	Lewis Stone
Buck McDougall	Francis J. MacDonald
Duncan McDougall	Melbourne McDowell
Old Roland	Spottiswood Aitken

The Penalty
Goldwyn (7) 11-15-20
Directed by Wallace Worsley
Scenario by Charles Kenyon and Philip Lonergan from novel by Gouverneur Morris.
Photographer Don Short
Cast:

Blizzard	Lon Chaney
Barbara	Claire Adams
Wilmot	Kenneth Harlan
Doctor	Charles Clary
Rose	Ethel Grey Terry
Bubble	Edouard Trebaol
Lichtenstein	Milton Ross
Pete	James Mason

Outside the Law
Universal-Jewel (8) 1-6-21
Directed by Tod Browning
Adapted by Lucian Hubbard and Tod Browning from story by Tod Browning.
Photographer William Fildew
Cast:

Molly Madden (Silky Moll)	Priscilla Dean
Silent Madden	Ralph Lewis
Black Mike Silva	Lon Chaney
Dapper Bill Ballard	Wheeler Oakman
Chang Lo	E. A. Warren
"That Kid"	Stanley Goethals
Joe Wang	"Guess Who" (Chaney)
Morgan Spencer	Melbourne McDowell
Inspector	Wilton Taylor

For Those We Love
Goldwyn (6) 3-11-21
Directed by Arthur Rosson
Scenario by Arthur Rosson from an original story by Perley Poore Sheehan.
Cast:

Trix Ulner	Lon Chaney
Bernice Arnold	Betty Compson
Frank	Frank Campeau
Bert	George Cooper
Jimmy Arnold	Richard Rosson
Vida	Camille Astor
Dr. Bailee	Bert Woodruff
George Arnold	Harry Duffield
Johnny Fletcher	Walter Morosco

Bits of Life
Associated First National (6) 9-4-21
Directed by Marshall Neilan, James Flood, William Scully
Scenario by Lucita Squier from stories by Hugh Wiley, Walter Trumbell, Thomas McMorrow, Marshall Neilan.
Cast:

Wesley Barry, John Bowers, Teddy Sampson, Dorothy Mackail, Edythe Chapman, Frederick Burton, Lon Chaney, Noah Beery, James Bradbury Jr., Rockliffe Fellows, Tammany Young, Harriet Hammond, Anna May Wong, James Neill.

The third of the four stories comprising the film was "Hop," with Lon Chaney and Anna May Wong.

Ace of Hearts
Goldwyn (6) 10-21-21
Directed by Wallace Worsley
Scenario by Ruth Wightman from novel *The Purple Mask* by Gouverneur Morris.
Photographer Don Short
Cast:

Lilith	Leatrice Joy
Forrest	John Bowers
Farralone	Lon Chaney
Morgridge	Hardee Kirkland
Chemist	Edwin N. Wallack
The Menace	Raymond Hatton

The Trap
Universal-Jewel (6) 5-9-22
Directed by Robert Thornby
Scenario by George C. Hull from a story by Lon Chaney, Irving Thalberg, Lucian Hubbard.
Photographer Virgil Miller
Cast:

Gaspard	Lon Chaney
Benson	Alan Hale
Thalie	Dagmar Godowsky
The Boy	Stanley Goethals
The Teacher	Irene Rich
The Factor	Spottiswood Aitken
The Priest	Herbert Standing
Police Sergeant	Frank Campeau

Flesh and Blood
Irving Cummings (6) 8-27-22
Directed by Irving Cummings
From a story by Louis Duryea Lighton.
Cast:

David Webster	Lon Chaney
Detective Doyle	DeWitt Jennings
Li Fang	Noah Beery
Fletcher Burton	Ralph Lewis
Ted Burton	Jack Mulhall
The Angel Lady	Edith Roberts
The Prince	Togo Yamamoto
The Landlady	Kate Price
The Policeman	Wilfred Lucas

Voices of the City
Goldwyn (6) 8-20-22
Directed by Wallace Worsley
Scenario by Arthur F. Slatter from *The Night Rose* by Leroy Scott.
Cast:

Georgia Rodman	Leatrice Joy
O'Rourke	Lon Chaney
Graham	John Bowers
Jimmy	Cullen Landis
Clancy	Richard Tucker

Mary Rodman	Mary Warren
Mrs. Rodman	Edythe Chapman
Sally	Betty Schade
Pierson	M. B. "Lefty" Flynn
Courey	Milton Ross
Garrison	John Cossar

The Light in the Dark
Associated First National (7) 9-3-22
Directed by Clarence F. Brown
Scenario by William Dudley Pelley and Clarence Brown.
Photographer Alfred Ortlieb
Cast:

Bessie MacGregor	Hope Hampton
J. Warburton Ashe	E. K. Lincoln
Tony Pantelli	Lon Chaney
Mrs. Templeton Orrin	Teresa Maxwell Conover
Mrs. Callerty	Dorothy Walters
Detective Braenders	Charles Mussett
Peters	Edgar Norton
Jerusalem Mike	Dora Davidson

Shadows
Preferred Pictures (7) 11-5-22
Directed by Tom Forman
Scenario by Eve Unsell and Hope Loring from story *Ching, Ching, Chinaman* by Wilbur Daniel Steele.
Photographer Harry Perry
Cast:

Yen Sin	Lon Chaney
Sympathy Gibbs	Marguerite de La Motte
John Malden	Harrison Ford
Nate Snow	John Sainpolis
Daniel Gibbs	Walter Long
"Mister Bad Boy"	Buddy Messinger
Mary Brent	Priscilla Bonner
Emsy Nickerson	Frances Raymond

Oliver Twist
Associated First National (8) 11-5-22
Directed by Frank Lloyd

Scenario by Frank Lloyd and Harry Weil from novel by Charles Dickens.
Photographers Glenn McWilliams and Robert Martin
Cast:

Oliver Twist	Jackie Coogan
Fagin	Lon Chaney
Nancy Sikes	Gladys Brockwell
Bill Sikes	George Siegmann
Mr. Bumble	James Marcus
The Widow Corney	Aggie Herring
Mr. Brownlow	Lionel Belmore
The Artful Dodger	Edouard Trebaol
Charley Bates	Taylor Graves
Mr. Monks	Carl Stockdale
Noah Claypool	Lewis Sargent
Charlotte	Joan Standing
Mr. Sowerberry	Nelson McDowell
Mr. Grimwig	Joseph H. Hazleton
Toby Crackitt	Eddie Boland
Mrs. Bedwin	Florence Hale
Rose Maylie	Esther Ralston
Mrs. Maylie	Gertrude Claire

Quincy Adams Sawyer
Metro (8) 12-3-22
Directed by Clarence Badger
Scenario by Bernard McConville from the novel by Charles Felton Pidgin.
Photographer Rudolph Berquist
Cast:

Quincy Adams Sawyer	John Bowers
Alice Pettengill	Blanche Sweet
Obadiah Strout	Lon Chaney
Lindy Putnam	Barbara LaMarr
Abner Stiles	Elmo Lincoln
Mandy Skinner	Louise Fazenda
Nathaniel Sawyer	Joseph Dowling
Mrs. Putnam	Claire McDowell
Deacon Pettengill	Edward Connelly
Betsy Ann Ross	June C. Elvidge
Hiram Maxwell	Victor Potel

Samanthy	Gale Henry
Ben Bates	Hank Mann
Mrs. Sawyer	Kate Lester
Bob Wood	Billy Farney
Cobb Twins	{ Taylor Graves { Harry Depp

The Blind Bargain
Goldwyn (5) 12-10-22
Directed by Wallace Worsley
Scenario by J. G. Hawks from *The Octave of Claudius* by Barry Pain.
Photographer Norbert Brodin
Cast:

Dr. Lamb	Lon Chaney
Angela	Jacqueline Logan
Robert	Raymond McKee
Mrs. Sandell	Virginia True Boardman
Mrs. Lamb	Fontaine La Rue
Bessie	Aggie Herring
Angela's Mother	Virginia Madison

All the Brothers Were Valiant
Metro (7) 1-15-23
Directed by Irvin V. Willat
Scenario by Julien Josephson from novel by Ben Ames Williams.
Photographer Robert Kurrle
Cast:

Joel Shore	Malcolm McGregor
Priss Holt	Billie Dove
Mark Shore	Lon Chaney
Aaron Burnham	William H. Orlamond
Finch	Robert McKim
Varde	Robert Kortman
Morrell	Otto Brower
Hooper	Curt Rehfeld
Cook	William V. Mong
Tom	Leo Willis

While Paris Sleeps
Hodkinson (6) 1-21-23
Directed by Maurice Tourneur

Malcolm McGregor, Lon Chaney, Robert McKim, and Robert Kortman in Metro's 1923 **All the Brothers Were Valiant.**

(Made in 1920 at Paramount as *The Glory of Love*)
From *The Glory of Love* by "Pan" (the pseudonym of Leslie Beresford).
Photographer Rene Guissart
Cast:

Henri Santados	Lon Chaney
Bebe Larvache	Mildred Manning
Dennis O'Keefe	Jack Gilbert
His Father	Harden Kirtland
George Morier	J. Farrell MacDonald
Father Marionette	Jack F. MacDonald

The Shock
Universal-Jewel (7) 6-10-23
Directed by Lambert Hillyer

Quasimodo and Dom Claude (Nigel de Brulier) inside the Cathedral of Notre Dame.

Scenario by Charles Kenyon from a story by William Dudley Pelley.
Photographer D. W. Warren
Cast:

Wilse Dilling	Lon Chaney
Gertrude Hadley	Virginia Valli
Jack Cooper	Jack Mower
Mischa Hadley	William Welsh
John Cooper Sr.	Henry Barrows
Anne Vincent	Christine Mayo
Olaf Wismer	Harry Devere
Bill	John Beck
The Captain	Walter Long

The Hunchback of Notre Dame
Universal Super Jewel (12) 9-16-23
Directed by Wallace Worsley
Adapted by Perley Poore Sheehan from *Notre Dame de Paris* by
Victor Hugo.

Dorothy Mackaill and Lon Chaney in **The Next Corner.**

Photographers Tony Koruman, Robert Newhard
Cast:

Quasimodo	Lon Chaney
Esmeralda	Patsy Ruth Miller
Phoebus	Norman Kerry
Clopin	Ernest Torrence
Mme. de Gondelaurier	Kate Lester
Jehan	Brandon Hurst
Gringoire	Raymond Hatton
Louis XI	Tully Marshall
Dom Claude	Nigel de Brulier
King's Chamberlain	Edwin Wallack
Justice of the Court	John Cossar
M. Neufchatel	Harry L. Van Meter
Godule	Gladys Brockwell
Marie	Eulalie Jansen
Fleur de Lis	Winifred Bryson
M. le Torteru	Nick de Ruiz
Charmolu's assistant	W. Ray Myers
Josephus	William Parke Sr.

The Next Corner
Paramount (7) 3-20-24
Directed by Sam Wood
Scenario by Monte Katterjohn from novel and play by Kate Jordan.
Photographer Alfred Gilks
Cast:

Robert Maury	Conway Tearle
Juan Serafin	Lon Chaney
Elsie Maury	Dorothy Mackaill
Don Arturo	Ricardo Cortez
Nina Race	Louise Dresser
Countess Longueval	Remea Radzina
Paula Vrain	Dorothy Cumming
Julie	Mrs. Bertha Feducha
The Stranger	Bernard Seigel

The Phantom of the Opera
Universal-Jewel (10) 9-6-25
Directed by Rupert Julian

Erik and Christine Daae (Mary Philbin).

Scenario by Elliott J. Clawson from novel by Gaston Leroux.
Photographers Charles Van Enger, Milton Bridenbecker, Virgil Miller
Cast:

Erik (the Phantom)	Lon Chaney
Christine Daae	Mary Philbin
Raoul de Chagny	Norman Kerry
Florine Papillon	Snitz Edwards
Simon	Gibson Gowland
Phillippe de Chagny	John Sainpolis
Carlotta	Virginia Pearson
The Persian	Arthur Edmund Carewe
Mama Valerius	Edith Yorke
The Prompter	Anton Vavorka
Joseph Buquet	Bernard Seigel
La Sorelli	Olive Ann Alcorn

Faust	Edward Cecil
Mephistopheles	Alexander Bevani
Valentine	John Miljan
Martha	Grace Marvin
M. Richard (Manager)	George B. Williams
M. Moncharmin	
(Manager)	Bruce Covington
Retiring Manager	Cesare Gravina

The newly formed company was first called Metro-Goldwyn when it was formally dedicated in April of 1924. Sometime later Louis B. Mayer's name was added making it Metro-Goldwyn-Mayer. The first film of the new organization was *He Who Gets Slapped*.

He Who Gets Slapped
Metro-Goldwyn (7) 11-2-24

Ruth King, Lon Chaney, and Marc McDermott in **He Who Gets Slapped.**

Directed by Victor Seastrom
Scenario by Victor Seastrom and Carey Wilson from the play by
Leonid Andreyev.
Photographer Milton Moore
Cast:

"He"	Lon Chaney
Consuelo	Norma Shearer
Bezano	John Gilbert
Count Mancini	Tully Marshall
Baron Regnard	Marc McDermott
Tricaud	Ford Sterling
Clown	Clyde Cook
Briquet	Harvey Clarke
Zinida	Paulette Duval
He's Wife	Ruth King
Clown	Brandon Hurst
Clown	George Davis

The Monster
Metro-Goldwyn (6) 2-22-25
Directed by Roland West
Scenario by Willard Mack and Albert G. Kenyon from the play by
Crane Wilbur.
Photographer Hal Mohr
Cast:

Dr. Ziska	Lon Chaney
Betty Watson	Gertrude Olmsted
Watson's Head Clerk	Hallam Cooley
Under Clerk	Johnny Arthur
Constable	Charles A. Sellon
Caliban	Walter James
Daffy Dan	Knute Erickson
Rigo	George Austin
Luke Watson	Edward McWade
Mrs. Watson	Ethel Wales

The Unholy Three
Metro-Goldwyn-Mayer (7) 8-4-25
Directed by Tod Browning
Scenario by Waldemar Young from the novel by Clarence A. Robbins.

Hallam Cooley and Johnny Arthur being set upon by the strange inhabitants of the mad doctor's sanitarium (Walter James, Knute Erickson, Lon Chaney, and George Austin).

Victor McLaglan, Harry Earles, Mae Busch, and Lon Chaney.

William Haines, Lon Chaney, Claire McDowell in **The Tower of Lies.**

Photographer David Kesson
Cast:

Echo	Lon Chaney
Rosie O'Grady	Mae Busch
Hector McDonald	Matt Moore
Hercules	Victor McLaglan
Tweedledee	Harry Earles
Regan	Mathew Betz
Announcer	Walter Perry
Jeweler	John Merkyl
John Arlington	Charles Wellesley
Butler	Percy Williams
Mrs. Arlington	Marjorie Morton
Arlington baby	Violet Crane
Commissioner of Police	Lou Morrison

Judge	Edward Connelly
Attorney for Defense	William Humphreys
Prosecuting Attorney	A. E. Warren

The Tower of Lies
M-G-M (7) 9-28-25
Directed by Victor Seastrom
Scenario by Agnes Christine Johnston from *The Emperor of Portugallia* by Selma Lagerlof.
Photographer Percy Hilburn
Cast:

Goldie	Norma Shearer
Jan	Lon Chaney
Lars	Ian Keith
Katrina	Claire McDowell
August	William Haines
Erik	David Torrence

The Blackbird
M-G-M (7) 1-11-26
Directed by Tod Browning
Scenario by Waldemar Young from *The Mockingbird* by Tod Browning.
Photographer Percy Hilburn
Cast:

Blackbird and Bishop	Lon Chaney
Fifi	Renee Adoree
West End Bertie	Owen Moore
Limehouse Polly	Doris Lloyd
The Shadow	Andy MacLennon
Red	William Weston
A Sightseer	Eric Mayne
Bertie's No. 1 Man	Sidney Bracy
Bertie's No. 2 Man	Ernis S. Adams

The Road to Mandalay
M-G-M (7) 6-18-26
Directed by Tod Browning
Scenario by Elliott Clawson from a story by Tod Browning and Herman Mankiewicz.

Chaney and Renee Adoree in **The Blackbird.**

Lon Chaney and Henry B. Walthall in **The Road to Mandalay.**

Lon Chaney and William Haines in **Tell It to the Marines.**

Photographer Merritt Gerstad
Cast:

Singapore Joe	Lon Chaney
Priest	H. B. Walthall
The Admiral	Owen Moore
Joe's Daughter	Lois Moran
English Charlie Wing	Kamiyama Sojin
Pansy	Rose Langdon
Servant	John George

Tell It to the Marines
M-G-M (10) 12-24-26
Directed by George Hill
Story and scenario by E. George Schrayer.

Claude King, Lon Chaney as the middle-aged Wu, and Sonny Lee.

Photographer Ira Morgan
Cast:

Sgt. O'Hara	Lon Chaney
Pvt. Skeet Burns	William Haines
Norma Dale	Eleanor Boardman
Cpl. Madden	Eddie Gribbon
Zaya	Carmel Myers
Chinese Bandit Leader	Warner Oland
Native	Mitchell Lewis
Gen. Wilcox	Frank Currier
Harry	Maurice Karns

Mr. Wu
M-G-M (8) 5-16-27
Directed by William Nigh

Joan Crawford and Lon Chaney.

Scenario by Lorna Moon from the novel by Louise Jordan Miln based on the play by Henry M. Vernon and Harold Owen.
Photographer John Arnold
Cast:

Mr. Wu	Lon Chaney
Mrs. Gregory	Louise Dresser
Nang Ping	Renee Adoree
Mr. Gregory	Holmes Herbert
Basil Gregory	Ralph Forbes
Hilda Gregory	Gertrude Olmsted
Ah Wong	Mrs. Wong Wing
Mr. Muir	Claude King
Loo Song	Anna May Wong
Little Wu	Sonny Lu

The Unknown
M-G-M (7) 6-13-27
Directed by Tod Browning
Scenario by Waldemar Young from a story by Tod Browning.
Photographer Merritt B. Gerstad
Cast:

Alonzo	Lon Chaney
Malabar	Norman Kerry
Estrellita	Joan Crawford
Zanzi	Nick de Ruiz
Cojo	John George
Gypsy	Frank Lanning

Mockery
M-G-M (7) 8-13-27
Directed by Benjamin Christensen
Scenario by Bradley King from a story by Benjamin Christensen.
Photographer Merritt B. Gerstad
Cast:

Sergei	Lon Chaney
Dimitri	Ricardo Cortez
Tatiana	Barbara Bedford
Mr. Gaidaroff	Mack Swain
Mrs. Gaidaroff	Emily Fitzroy
Ivan	Charles Puffy
Butler	Kai Schmidt

Barbara Bedford, Ricardo Cortez, and Lon Chaney in **Mockery.**

London After Midnight
M-G-M (7) 12-17-27
Directed by Tod Browning
Scenario by Waldemar Young from *The Hypnotist* by Tod Browning.
Photographer Merritt B. Gerstad
Cast:

Burke	Lon Chaney
Lucille Balfour	Marcelline Day
Sir James Hamlin	Henry B. Walthall
Butler	Percy Williams
Arthur Hibbs	Conrad Nagel
Miss Smithson	Polly Moran
Bat Girl	Edna Tichenor
The Stranger	Claude King

Conrad Nagel, Lon Chaney, H. B. Walthall, Marcelline Day, and Polly Moran in
London After Midnight.

The Big City
M-G-M (8) 3-24-28
Directed by Tod Browning
Scenario by Waldemar Young from a story by Tod Browning.
Cast:

Chuck Collins	Lon Chaney
Sunshine	Marcelline Day
Curly	James Murray
Helen	Betty Compson
Red	Matthew Betz
The Arab	John George
Tennessee	Virginia Pearson
Grogan	Walter Percival
O'Hara	Lew Short
Blinkie	Eddie Sturgis

Laugh, Clown, Laugh
M-G-M (8) 4-14-28
Directed by Herbert Brenon
Scenario by Elizabeth Meehan from the play by David Belasco and Tom Cushing based on the Italian play *Ridi, Pagliacci* by Fausto Martino.
Photographer James Wong Howe
Cast:

Tito	Lon Chaney
Simon	Bernard Seigel
Simonetta	Loretta Young
Giacinta	Cissy Fitzgerald
Luigi	Nils Asther
Diane	Gwen Lee

Chaney as the crook in **The Big City** dresses in the latest fashion for the part. His confidant is James Murray.

"Laugh, clown, laugh!"

Mae Busch and Lon Chaney in **While the City Sleeps.**

While the City Sleeps
M-G-M (9) 10-20-28
Directed by Jack Conway
Story and scenario by A. P. Younger.
Photographer Henry Sharp
Cast:

Dan	Lon Chaney
Myrtle	Anita Page
Marty	Carroll Nye
Skeeter	Wheeler Oakman
Bessie	Mae Busch
Mrs. McGinnis	Polly Moran
Mrs. Sullivan	Lydia Yeamans Titus
Dwiggins	William Orlamond
Wally	Richard Carle

West of Zanzibar
M-G-M (7) 12-24-28
Directed by Tod Browning
Scenario by Elliott Clawson from the play *Kongo* by Charles de
Vonde and Kilbourn Gordon.
Photographer Percy Hilburn
Cast:

Phroso	Lon Chaney
Crane	Lionel Barrymore
Doc	Warner Baxter
Maizie	Mary Nolan
Anna	Jacqueline Gadsdon
Tiny	Roscoe Ward
Babe	Kalla Pasha
Bumbu	Curtis Nero

Where East Is East
M-G-M (7) 5-4-29
Directed by Tod Browning
Scenario by Richard Schayer from a story by Tod Browning and
Harry Sinclair Drago.
Cast:

Tiger Haynes	Lon Chaney
Toyo	Lupe Velez
Mme. De Silva	Estelle Taylor

Chaney in the disguise of a circus freak in **West of Zanzibar.**

Bobby Bailey	Lloyd Hughes
Padre	Louis Stern
Ming	Mrs. Wong Wing

Thunder
M-G-M (9) 7-8-29
Directed by William Nigh
Scenario by Ann Price and Byron Morgan from a story by Byron Morgan.
Photographer Henry Sharp
Cast:

Grumpy Anderson	Lon Chaney
Tommy	James Murray

Estelle Taylor and Lon Chaney.

Louis Stern, Lon Chaney, Lupe Velez, and Lloyd Hughes in **Where East Is East.**

Lon Chaney, Phyllis Haver, Wally Albright Jr., James Murray, George Duryea, and Frances Morris in **Thunder.**

Ivan Linow, Lila Lee, Lon Chaney, and Harry Earles.

Zella	Phyllis Haver
Jim	George Duryea
Molly	Frances Morris
Davey	Wally Albright Jr.

The Unholy Three
M-G-M (8) 7-2-30
Directed by Jack Conway
Scenario by J. C. and Elliot Nugent from the novel by Clarence Robbins.
Photographer Percy Hilburn
Cast:

Echo	Lon Chaney
Rosie	Lila Lee
Hector	Elliot Nugent
Midget	Harry Earles
Prosecuting Attorney	John Miljan
Hercules	Ivan Linow
Regan	Clarence Burton
Defense Attorney	Crauford Kent

Chronology

1883—April 1, Alonzo Chaney born at Colorado Springs, Colorado, to Frank and Clara Hennessey Chaney.

1892—Withdrawn from fourth grade to care for invalid mother.

1895—Worked as prop boy in local theatre for twenty-five cents a night.

Worked as a Pike's Peak guide during summer months.

1898—Father sent him to Denver to learn carpet-laying and wall-papering trades.

1901—Brother John formed own stock company. Lon joined and stayed on when brother sold the company, touring for several years.

1905—May 31, married Cleva Creighton, Oklahoma City.

1906—February, son, Creighton Tull, born.

1909—Stage manager for Kolb and Dill in San Francisco; Chaney and Cleva separated.

1912—Chaney entered movies.

1914—Divorced from Cleva. (April)

1915—Universal City opened. Chaney became regular member of studio's stock company.

Married Hazel Hastings.

1917—Gained recognition in *Hell Morgan's Girl*.

1918—Left Universal to become free-lance actor.

Scored in William S. Hart's *Riddle Gawne*.

1919—Approached star status in *The Miracle Man*.

1920—*The Penalty*.

1923—Star of *The Hunchback of Notre Dame*.

1924—April, M-G-M formally dedicated at Culver City.
First film at new studio, *He Who Gets Slapped*, with Chaney as star.

1925—*The Phantom of the Opera* at Universal.

1930—Made first talking picture, *The Unholy Three*.
August 20, entered St. Vincent's Hospital for first of three blood transfusions because of hemorrhage.
August 26, died.
August 27, buried at Forest Lawn.

Index to Text

Index to Illustrations